MIND IN NATURE

NOBEL CONFERENCE XVII

Gustavus Adolphus College, St. Peter, Minnesota

MIND IN NATURE

Edited by

RICHARD Q. ELVEE

With Contributions by

John Archibald Wheeler, Sir Karl Popper,
Richard Rorty, Ragnar Granit, Eugene Wigner,
and Wolfhart Pannenberg

1817

Harper & Row, Publishers, San Francisco

Cambridge, Hagerstown, New York, Philadelphia
London, Mexico City, Saõ Paulo, Sydney

FIRST EDITION

Designer: Jim Mennick

Library of Congress Cataloging in Publication Data

Nobel Conference (17th : 1981 : Gustavus Adolphus College)
  MIND IN NATURE

  1. Thought and thinking—Congresses. 2. Knowledge, Theory of—Congresses. 3. Reason—Congresses. 4. Physics—Philosophy—Congresses. 5. Philosophy of nature—Congresses. I. Elvee, Richard Q. (Richard Quentin). II. Wheeler, John Archibald, 1911– . III. Title.
  BD161.N6 1981   128'.2   82–48155
  ISBN 0–06–250285–9

---

82   83   84   85   86   10   9   8   7   6   5   4   3   2   1

To Russell and Patricia Lund,
friends of culture

Contents

Preface

The Nobel Committee concludes each year's lectures with a festive dinner followed by conversations that review the Conference. It is a family affair for those who come from many separate institutions to share the annual event.

After this year's dinner, in the darkening commons, I was approached by a high school boy, smooth faced and bright eyed, young in the way high school "physicists" are young. He informed me, excitedly, that this Conference on "Mind in Nature" was the highest point of his life. He was old enough, I mused, to know that life ebbed and flowed, but too young to know how few times a high cultural tide would flow in and fill everything.

I was pleased with this encounter, for the Conference had envisaged just such high school scientists as those to be enlightened and encouraged by the proceedings, in order that the state's most precious scientific resource, the minds of its children, would not be lost to the sciences. I reflected, too, on how many of these students from Minnesota towns and cities whom we first glimpsed along the college walks during the brief Nobel days we recognized again during their Gustavus years and eventually saw matriculated in the graduate schools of America and Europe, taking their places in the larger scientific community.

These were good thoughts, good feelings. I breathed a director's thanks to the Russell Lunds; to Minnesota and its high school science faculties; to Gustavus Adolphus College and the Nobel Foundation; to Robert Peterson, Elaine Brostrom, Jeanie Reese, and Julie Lloyd of Gustavus Adolphus College; and to Clayton Carlson of the house of Harper for this volume. I turned then with anticipation to Nobel XVIII, ''Darwin's Legacy,'' a conference that would bring Stephen Jay Gould, E. O. Wilson, Sir Peter Medawar, Richard Leakey, Irving Stone, and Jaroslav Pelikan to the campus for another Oktoberfest.

RICHARD QUENTIN ELVEE
Program Director
The Nobel Conference

Introduction

The papers and conversations included in this volume were originally presented during the two days of Nobel Conference XVII, October 6 and 7, 1981, on the campus of Gustavus Adolphus College in St. Peter, Minnesota. The Conference is the outcome of an association between the Nobel Foundation of Stockholm and a private American college founded by Swedish immigrants in the 1860s. In 1963, the college dedicated its hall of science as the American memorial to Alfred Nobel, with twenty-six laureates in attendance. Two years later, the Foundation endorsed the organization of a conference in which scientists and members of other disciplines could meet to discuss leading topics in science, for the benefit of a large public audience. With the passing years, the original promise of the conference has been richly fulfilled by a series which, by 1981, numbered seventeen, and which brought to the campus six of the world's great minds, a host of professors, students, and citizens from throughout the American Midwest, numbering in all about 3500.

The 1981 topic, "The Place of Mind in Nature," originated in the conversations of Gustavus physicists and theologians wishing to explore further the revolution in physical thought that was moving the mind and the apparatus of the human observer to the center of the inquiry about the ultimate nature of things. Physicists John Wheeler and Eugene Wigner were invited to address the immediate issue of the implications of quantum mechanics for reflective thought on the question. The inquiry was expanded to include the idea of the "emergent mind" in the philosophy of Sir Karl Popper, and the work of the neurophysicist Ragnar Granit, and eventually the concept of "Spirit-Mind" in the theology of Wolfhart Pannenberg. Finally, philosopher Richard Rorty was invited as a positivist control on the potentially out-of-hand speculations about the mind.

In the main, the intentions of the organizers were realized: to assemble diverse intellectual worldviews at a single table, permitting those who gathered to hear a rich, if often controversial, exchange about the nature of the mind. If, at times, the positions held were so disparate that communication was impossible, each participant valiantly opened a path to the others, and the large audience was rewarded with an intellectual exchange of a very high order and an opportunity to see the contrast in positions as different as Rorty's materialism and Pannenberg's idealism. Above all, the six major lectures here offered in print were statements of a quality that deserved this larger forum; whether summations of a lifetime's work or fundamental statements in a developing oeuvre.

In the keynote lecture, John Wheeler recounts in a unique reminiscence the momentous dialogue between Einstein and Wheeler's teacher, Niels Bohr, which had such consequences for physical thought in the twentieth century. This is followed by his unique ideas concerning the elementary quantum phenomenon, "a mysterious new entrant on the stage of physics," whereby the observer-participant is more basic than particle or fields as an explanation of the "big bang" or the "entirety of existence."

In the second lecture, Eugene Wigner reviews the history of physics from Newton to quantum, showing how each extension of ideas altered the principles of the earlier theories, and how radical a departure was the quantum theory. He explains his ideas of the "approximate validity" of the laws of nature, and the lack of harmony between quantum mechanics and general relativity. Particularly is he concerned with the limitations of current physical theory for a description of consciousness.

For his part, Richard Rorty argues for dispensing with the concept of mind as the "blur" with which Western intellectuals became obsessed, after they had given up on "God" as an explanatory concept. At length he describes his opposition to the "intuitionism" of philosophers Nagel and Searle, and defends the Ryle-Dennett "tradition" of verificationism. "Cognitive applies to whatever the best account of cognition leads the psychologists to call a cognitive process." He criticizes Russell, Whitehead, James, and Dewey for thinking that ordinary vulgar materialism was not enough. "We should just stop being afraid of science and of vulgar materialism. We should substitute the question, 'What further descriptions of ourselves do we need, in addition to those with which science provides us?' for the question, 'What knowledge of ourselves can theologians or philosophers give us which scientists cannot give?'" He concludes by proposing that beyond the vocabularies useful for prediction and control —the sciences—there are vocabularies of moral and political life, and of the arts, and that human beings are the poetic species, who change themselves by changing their behavior.

Ragnar Granit, in an elegant, richly illustrated paper, speaks of mind as an emergent property in the evolution of life—a hierarchic biological system exhibiting a creative resourcefulness for which a "typical fragmentary analysis in a science such as chemistry has not the arsenal of concepts." Mind, he asserts, is a psychological dictator that rules by order-giving and pays no attention to the chemical machinery employed, and finally considers that evolution has put a premium on the development of "intended action" in human beings.

In a remarkable paper, which owing to illness Sir Karl Popper was unable to deliver at the conference, the great philosopher sums up his many reflections upon the "Place of Mind." His arguments, not unfamiliar and always challenging, receive a forceful articulation in a paper that will be read and reread by anyone interested in the subject.

In sum, Karl Popper conjectures that the beginnings of mindlike behavior can be found very early in evolution; that, with the emergence of exploratory behavior, mindlike behavior plays an increasingly active part in evolution; that an organism may search for a friendly environment; that mind-like behavior turns into conscious behavior and the human mind evolves in an evolutionary process in which the emerging mind plays an active part, so that we become largely makers of ourselves; that our minds are largely responsible for our place in nature; that the human mind is essentially a problem solver, and the most important step in its evolution was that from a signaling language to a descriptive language; that, ultimately, the human mind (in Popper's terms, World 2), in constant interaction with nature (World 1), and its own artifacts such as science, arts, and architecture (World 3), continues to transcend itself—the most important fact of all evolution.

In the final paper, theologian Wolfhart Pannenberg follows Karl Popper's suggestion that language, once created, exerted the selection pressure under which the human mind emerged, so that the emergence of self-conscious mind is based on language. Pannenberg then describes language as an ecstatic event that originates in a "spiritual field." He attempts to show how mythical and religious spirituality surround the first origins of language in the history of the human race and the importance for language of its basis in Spirit. After a lengthy discussion of the meanings of "mind" and "spirit" in the biblical and patristic literature, he offers several wide-reaching proposals: that one may explain the fact that the human mind and language are fit to grasp the reality of things as they really are, on the assumption that the human mind and nature share a common spiritual origin; that the structures of living being and the activity of the human mind have a common rootage in the "spirit"; and that there is in all life a self-transcending integrative process in which the human mind shares, which transcends the individual human mind.

Contributors

JOHN ARCHIBALD WHEELER
Joseph Henry Professor Emeritus of Physics, Princeton University; Ashbel Smith Professor of Physics, University of Texas, Austin. Albert Einstein Prize 1965; Enrico Fermi Award 1968; The Franklin Medal 1969; National Medal of Science 1971.

SIR KARL RAIMUND POPPER
Professor Emeritus of Logic and Scientific Method, University of London. Fellow of the Royal Society 1976; Fellow of the British Academy 1958; Sonning Prize, University of Copenhagen 1973; Lippincott Award, USA 1976; Prize of the City of Vienna 1978; Prize of the University of Tubingen; Germany 1981. Among the books translated in 22 languages: *The Poverty of Historicism* (1957), *The Logic of Scientific Discovery* (1959), *Conjectures and Refutations* (1963), *Objective Knowledge* (1972), *The Self and Its Brain* (1977).

RICHARD RORTY
Kenan Professor of Humanities, University of Virginia; Fellow of the American Council of Learned Societies 1969; Guggenheim Fellow 1973–74. Author of *Philosophy and the Mirror of Nature* (1979).

RAGNAR ARTHUR GRANIT
Professor Emeritus of Neurophysiology and Director, Neurophysiological Department, Medical Nobel Institute, Royal Caroline Institute, Stockholm; Royal Swedish Academy; Royal Society of London; American Philosophical Society; National Academy of Sciences USA, Nobel Laureate in Medicine 1967.

EUGENE PAUL WIGNER
Thomas D. Jones Professor Emeritus of Physics, Princeton University. Enrico Fermi Award 1958; Max Planck Medal 1961; National Medal of Science 1969; Albert Einstein Award 1972; Nobel Laureate in Physics 1963.

WOLFHART PANNENBERG
Professor of Systematic Theology, Munich University; Bavarian Academy of Sciences 1977. Major books: *Revelation as History* (1969); *What is Man* (1970), *Jesus—God and Man* (1969), *Basic Questions in Theology* (1971), *The Apostles Creed* (1972), *Theology and the Philosophy of Science* (1978).

Bohr, Einstein, and the Strange Lesson of the Quantum*

JOHN ARCHIBALD WHEELER

Gustavus Adolphus colleagues and friends, the death today of President Anwar Sadat reminds us once again that great causes make great men. We will not easily forget this hero of statesmanship, a man who worked with all the force of his life for a cause greater than himself: justice through negotiation.

Neither can we forget, especially on this day and at this meeting, two heroes of science, Niels Bohr and his seven-years older colleague Albert Einstein (Figure 1), who worked with all the force of their lives for something greater than themselves: "a completely harmonious account of existence." Bohr, in the words engraved on Princeton's Putnam monument to him, we honor as "Elucidator of the structure of the atom, elucidator of the structure of the nucleus, author of the principle of complementarity." Einstein we venerate for discovering that light acts like particles, for bringing together space and time into spacetime, and for showing us that gravitation is not some strange and foreign influence propagated through space, but a manifestation of the curvature of space geometry itself.

* Opening lecture of Nobel Conference XVII, "The Place of Mind in Nature," presented at Gustavus Adolphus College, St. Peter, Minnesota, October 6 and 7, 1981, as revised for publication. Preparation for publication assisted by the Center for Theoretical Physics, University of Texas at Austin, and NSF Grant PHY7826592.

Figure 1. Niels Bohr and Albert Einstein in discussion during their week-long visit at the home of Paul Ehrenfest in Leyden in 1933, not long before Ehrenfest's death. Six years earlier Ehrenfest, in tears, had told his friend Samuel Goudsmit of the continuing disagreement between the two colleagues he admired so much, adding that he had to make a choice between Bohr's and Einstein's positions, and that he could not but agree with Bohr.

Photographs by Paul Ehrenfest. Restoration of negatives and print production by William R. Whipple. Photo courtesy of the American Institute of Physics Niels Bohr Library.

The Bohr-Einstein Dialogue

Heroes as they were to all the world, they were also always heroes to each other, even though they did not meet until the younger, Bohr, was thirty-six. After the meeting, Einstein wrote, "I am studying your great works and—when I get stuck anywhere—now have the pleasure of seeing your friendly young face before me smiling and explaining." And Niels Bohr, in his turn, spoke many a time of his admiration for the depth and penetrating power of Einstein. How does it come about then that these two men could disagree so fundamentally and so long as they did, from 1927 to Einstein's death in 1955, about the meaning and message of the quantum and its consequences for how we should perceive the world?

It is of no use in understanding this debate to know that quantum theory is the overarching principle of twentieth-century physics. It is of no use to know that it provides a system of equations by which we can predict the motions of electrons in atoms, the binding of molecules, the physics of superconductivity, the fission of uranium, and the breakup of new particles. The point at issue between the two men had nothing to do with equations. It had rather to do with the nature of "reality" itself. To Einstein, the world existed "out there." To Bohr, the observer's choice of his observing equipment had inescapable and normally unpredictable consequences for what will be found.

That there would ever be a point of fundamental disagreement, and still less, that it would concern the very nature of "reality," was not clear in the first quarter of the century of the development of quantum theory. In that period, the quantum work of Bohr and Einstein almost makes a duet. In 1900 Max Planck, destined through his work and character to become the father figure of German physics, had discovered that the energy of an electromagnetic wave of a given color confined in a box could not take on any arbitrary value. Instead, its energy is like one's footstep on a ladder. It is an integral multiple of a basic unit. This unit, Q, depends on the color of the light, but for light of any given color, has an ever-constant value. The amount of energy in the light of that color can be zero, or Q, or 2Q, or 3Q, or 27Q, or 144Q, but never, for example, 4.37Q. In other words, the energy comes in "hunks," the English equivalent for the wartime German use of "quantum of bread" or "quantum of margarine" to denote the fixed ration in times of shortage. One who wishes to take some of the mystery out of the words, "quantum theory of electromagnetic radiation" can call it the "hunk theory of light."

Does "God Play Dice"?

Open a tiny hole in the box and let some of the light of a given color escape and spread out. Then the luminous energy in its travel will also be divided in hunks—"quanta" (or "photons," as Gilbert N. Lewis was later to name them)—each random in its direction of travel and time of arrival. This was the picture that Einstein gave the world in 1905. This was the way he explained the previously puzzling observations of the so-called photoelectric effect, the ejection of electrons from metal by light. The weakness or the brightness of the light, Einstein explained, affects the number of hunks of energy raining down on the metal and the number of electrons that will be ejected from the metal, but in no way alters the ability of the individual hunk to do the ejecting. Einstein won the Nobel Prize for this work. He had also put a cloud, however small, into what before had been the bright blue deterministic sky of physics. The very man who from 1928 onward was to say so many times, "God does not play dice," was the first to show that "God does play dice." No way could be found to predict when and where a quantum of electromagnetic energy would hit.

If the explanation of the photoelectric effect was the first movement in the early Bohr-Einstein duet, the long, slow unveiling of the lesson of the quantum, Bohr's 1913 theory of the structure of the atom was the second. He was not concerned about circular and elliptic orbits of electrons in atoms. He was concerned why matter, composed as it is out of mutually attracting positively and negatively charged particles, does not all collapse in a microscopic fraction of a second, radiating away enormous energy into space. He found himself forced to conclude that the atom cannot have any arbitrary energy; it can have only one or another "characteristic" energy value or "energy eigen" value or be only in one or another "stationary" energy level or "stationary" state, not equally spaced like the steps in the ladder of electromagnetic energy. The atom can give out radiation only by jumping from a state of higher energy to a state of lower energy. But to which state the atom jumps, and when it jumps, are utterly beyond prediction, purely probabilistic. The black cloud of chance had spread further over the previously clear deterministic sky of physics.

In movement three of the duet, in 1916, Einstein explained how the laws of chance apply as well to the absorption of light as to its emission and as well to radioactivity—this chance emission of a particle from an atomic nucleus—as to the jump of an atomic electron from one state of motion to another.

In movement four, in 1927, Bohr, going beyond work done earlier that year by Werner Heisenberg, stated in terms of new generality why it would never be possible to observe or predict the detailed course of any atomic jump. He put the central point in his principle of complementarity, "Any given application of classical concepts precludes the simultaneous use of other classical concepts which in a different connection are equally necessary for the elucidation of the phenomena."

Nothing sounds more mysterious on one's first airing it. No wonder that at first workers in Paris, speaking of what was going on in Copenhagen, referred to "la brume du nord," the fog from the north. No wonder that many a respectable physicist in Germany resolved to pay no attention to this new development. No wonder that Erwin Schrödinger, author of the quantum theory equation describing what happens to the electron in an atom, hearing on a visit to Copenhagen all about Heisenberg's principle of "indeterminism" or "uncertainty" and of its generalization in Bohr's principle of complementarity, said, "If I had known all this Herumspringerei, all this jumping about, to which my equation was going to give rise, I would never have had anything to do with it in the first place." No wonder Einstein referred to these new developments, in a letter to his friend Max Born, as the "Bohr-Heisenberg tranquilizing philosophy." Here the two men parted ways. Einstein, dismayed by now at the consequences of "God plays dice," reverted to the deterministic philosophy of his great hero, Bernard Spinoza, and argued thereafter that "God does not play dice."

Thus 1927 marked the end of the duet and the beginning of the twenty-eight-year dialogue. It ended only at the death of Einstein. In the first phase of the dialogue, Einstein, who had himself contributed so vitally to quantum theory, attempted to show that it was logically inconsistent. Every idealized experiment that he brought up to make this point, however, Bohr turned around to stress with renewed force the inescapability of quantum theory. In the second phase of the debate, which began in 1933, the year of Einstein's removal to America, he tried to show that quantum theory was incompatible with any reasonable idea of "reality." To this Bohr replied, in effect, "your idea of reality is too limited."

What is the right idea of "reality"? That is a deeper question. Not Bohr, not anyone, has yet the answer. Mankind through its agent, physics, is now on a long but exciting road of discovery. But, Bohr tells us in effect, no one can take even the first steps of the way who is not guided by the lesson of the quantum. In turn, no one can truly appreciate the lesson of the quantum who is not aware of the issue in the great debate—and its outcome.

In all the history of human thought in recent centuries, it is difficult to point to a dialogue between two greater men extending over a longer time on a deeper issue at a higher level of colleagueship.

The Split-Beam Experiment

Of all the idealized experiments taken up by the two friends in their effort to win agreement, none was simpler than the beam splitter (Figure 2). The question posed by the experiment seems straightforward. What is the track followed by a single photon, a single quantum of light, a single hunk of electromagnetic energy on its way from the point of entry on the left to the point of registration of its arrival in one or the other of the two photodetectors on the right?

The conclusion of the great debate is devastating. It is wrong even to raise the question. It is wrong to talk of the track of the quantum. We have no right to say what it is doing in all of its long travel from point of entry to point of detection. We have to deal instead with a new feature of nature, an *elementary quantum phenomenon* with a paradoxical feature: "No elementary quantum phenomenon is a phenomenon until it is a registered phenomenon"—that is to say, brought to a close by an irreversible act of amplification such as the triggering of a photodetector or the initiation of an avalanche of electrons in a geiger counter, or the blackening of a grain of photographic emulsion.

Can't one stick one's finger in and find out where the quantum went on its way from entry to photodetector? Of course! But then one has a new phenomenon and has reached no closer than before to its center. In other words, an "elementary quantum phenomenon" is extended in space and time. It is non-localizable. Above all, it is untouchable, impenetrable, impalpable. It is a mysterious new entrant on the stage of physics. For all we know, it may someday turn out to be the fundamental building unit of all that is, more basic even than particles or fields of force or space and time themselves. But that is an issue for the future. Here we are asking

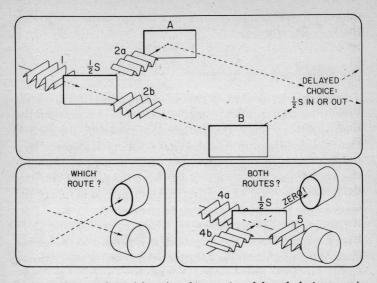

Figure 2. Beam splitter (above) and its use in a delayed-choice experiment (below). An electromagnetic wave comes in at 1 and encounters the half-silvered mirror marked ½S that splits it into two beams, 2A and 2B, of equal intensity, which are reflected by mirrors A and B to a crossing point at the right. Counters (lower left) located past the point of crossing tell by which route an arriving photon has come. In the alternative arrangement (lower right), a half-silvered mirror is inserted at the point of crossing. On one side it brings beams 4A and 4B into destructive interference, so that the counter located on that side never registers anything. On the other side the beams are brought into constructive interference to reconstitute a beam, 5, of the original strength, 1. Every photon that enters at 1 is registered in that second counter in the idealized case of perfect mirrors and 100 percent photodetector efficiency.

Here is a wrong way of speaking about the experiment: In the one arrangement (lower left), one finds out by which route the photon came. In the other arrangement (lower right), one has evidence that the arriving photon came by both routes. (In the new "delayed-choice" version of the experiment, one decides whether to put in the half-silvered mirror or to take it out at the very last minute. Thus one decides whether the photon "shall have come by one route, or by both routes" after it has "already done its travel.")

The right way to speak about the experiment is quite different: No questions that are simpler, but challenging enough. What is there about this split-beam experiment that forces one to recognize this new entrant on the scene of physics? Why did Einstein reject it? And what clues does it give us about the nature of reality?

Is it really a mistaken idea to ask for the track of the photon through the split-beam apparatus? And, before that, what is the mysterious action of the second half-silvered mirror in Figure 2 that it reduces to zero any radiation going to one of the counters? Both questions invite us to look a little more closely at the split-beam experiment. What would happen at the second half-silvered mirror if beam 4A alone struck it is quite clear. Half of the photons in that beam would go straight through from back to front and hit the more forward of the two counters. The other half of the quanta of energy would be reflected by the very thin silver coating into the more remote counter. No astonishment there! Or, if we blocked beam 4A and admitted beam 4B alone, say with fifty quanta in it, to strike the mirror from the front, we would once again have the result that twenty-five of the photons, more or less (statistical fluctuation!), would hit the one counter, and twenty-five less or more, would hit the other. Something new happens when both beams are there: "interference." More gives less! In the space between the mirror and the rear counter, the reflected part of 4A and the transmitted part of 4B are both present. Does that double the number of counts? No, it reduces it to zero. The crests of the transmitted part of 4B and the troughs of the reflected part of 4A lie on top of each other; the two waves cancel out. This "destructive interference" kills the electromagnetic field in that region. That is how it comes about that the rear counter gets nothing. In contrast, in the space between the mirror and the front

---

elementary quantum phenomenon *is* a phenomenon until it is a recorded phenomenon—that is, registered or "observed," or detected by an irreversible act of amplification, here the triggering of the one or the other photodetector.

counter, we have "constructive interference." The crests of the reflected part of 4B coincide with the crests of the transmitted part of 4A. The resulting total wave, 5, in that region has twice the amplitude and four times the intensity that either beam alone would give. The forward counter receives not $25 + 25 = 50$ quanta, but $4 \times 25 = 100$ hunks of energy.

This destruction of the radiation going toward the rear counter, and otherwise unexpected buildup of the radiation going toward the front counter—this destructive and constructive interference—is no dream. It has been checked by the tens of thousands of students who have used an interferometer for optical measurements. It is impossible to explain this interference except by saying that the radiation travels both routes.

Very well, then, why not say that a fact is a fact; say that every quantum of radiant energy that hits the forward counter (when the second half-silvered mirror is in place) has come by both routes? The indivisible hunk of energy divides! Is not this preposterous conclusion, Einstein argued,* direct evidence that quantum theory is logically self-contradictory? And can't the contradiction be made all the more evident? We have only to remove the half-silvered mirror and let the light arrive one photon at a time, minutes or hours apart. Then how can we escape from saying that a photon which sets off the front counter has traveled by route A? And one that sets off the rear counter has arrived exclusively by route B? What nonsense to have to say that a photon travels by one route, but travels by both routes; and to have to add, it travels by both routes but it only travels by one route!

Bohr's Principle of Complementarity

Bohr explained that one is dealing with two different ex-

---

* The center of discussion in the Bohr-Einstein dialogue was more often the so-called double-slit experiment than the beam splitter depicted in Figure 2. The latter is made the focus of attention here because it presents the central point without getting into the physics of interference patterns.

periments. In one, the "which route?" experiment, the half-silvered mirror is removed. In the other, the "both route" experiment, the half-silvered mirror is in place. It is physically impossible to do both experiments at the same time, to have the mirror both there and not there. We ourselves make the choice as to which way we will do the experiment. In the one way of doing the experiment we gain some information about the "where" of the photon—that is, a particle property of the quantum. In the other way of doing the experiment we learn something about an interference property of the photon —that is, its wave character. But nature is so built that we cannot do both at once. That is what Bohr means by the principle of complementarity. We can devise an experiment that brings into evidence the particle character of light, or one that brings into evidence the wave nature of light. But we cannot devise an experiment that will bring both features into evidence at the same time.

Wave and particle are not contradictory terms for a photon. They are complementary. Nature sees to it that "any given application of the classical concept" of wave automatically "precludes the simultaneous use of the classical concept" of particle. Both concepts are needed for a complete under-standing of the full range of do-able experiments; but there is no one experiment in which a clean and clear application can be made of both ideas.

Bohr deeply felt that complementarity is one of the most central of all features of nature. In later life, called on by the Danish government to receive the Danish order of nobility, obliged to construct a coat of arms, he chose for its device the famous yin-yang symbol of the Orient (Figure 3). A curved line divides a circle into two parts, forever separate but forever juxtaposed. It symbolized our freedom to deal with one aspect of nature but at the cost of being unable to deal at the same time with the complementary aspects. He hoped the idea of complementarity in time would be taught in every secondary school, as guide not only to physics but to all of life. You can deal with your small boy who has set fire to a

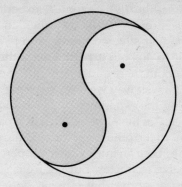

Figure 3. The ancient yin-yang emblem, used by Bohr to symbolize complementarity.

neighbor's shrubbery in a spirit of justice, or in a spirit of love; but it is impossible to apply consistently both approaches at the same time. It is acceptable to conceive of what goes on in the brain in deterministic terms, and equally acceptable to conceive of it in terms of free will; but to apply consistently both outlooks at the same time is out of the question. "Non contraria sunt, sed complementaria," Bohr chose as motto for his coat of arms: "Not contradictory, but complementary."

Einstein could not accept this "tranquilizing philosophy." He felt it was incompatible with any reasonable idea of reality to make what we find depend on what we choose to study. He struggled to find an experiment that would expose what he felt to be the unreasonableness of the quantum theory account of reality. In 1935, Einstein with Boris Podolsky and Nathan Rosen proposed what they thought to be a crucial experiment. In it, what happens at point A depends or appears to depend on what one does at some other point B from which, nevertheless, there is no way to signal to A. In the meantime, experiments of this "Einstein, Podolsky, Rosen" type have been done in significant variety and in numerous laboratories. Always the result agrees with quantum theory.

The "Delayed-Choice" Experiment

In many ways the simplest "Einstein, Podolsky, Rosen" experiment that one can do is one that I have called a "delayed-choice experiment." No example lies closer to hand than the "split-beam experiment" itself, modified in one small but vital respect. We no longer make the decision whether to put in the second half-silvered mirror or take it out before we do the experiment on the photon. Instead, we insert it or remove it in the very last fraction of a nanosecond (10^{-9} sec; light goes 1 foot in a nanosecond) before the photon arrives. We, by our last minute decision, determine whether the photon shall travel "one of the two routes" or "both routes"—to use a misleading and unacceptable language—*after* the photon has *already* accomplished that travel! Quantum mechanics seem at first sight to make "what has already happened" in the past depend on a choice made in the present!

Phenomenon

Bohr had to introduce a new word to make clear the central point, or rather a new use of the old word, "phenomenon." Bohr emphasized that it is completely wrong to use such terms as "the track of the photon" and the photon travels "both routes." We have no right to say anything about what the photon is doing in its passage from the point of entry to the point of reception. Nothing has happened until it has happened. No elementary quantum phenomenon *is* a phenomenon until it is a registered phenomenon, a phenomenon brought to a close by an irreversible act of amplification. When we change the observing equipment we do not learn more about that phenomenon. We have instead a phenomenon that is new and different. The observer's choice of what he shall look for has an inescapable consequence for what he will find.

Decide Now "What Shall Have Happened" Billions of Years in the Past?

The split-beam experiment in the delayed-choice version reaches back into the past in apparent opposition to the normal order of time; but how far back? The distance of travel in a laboratory split-beam experiment might be 30 meters, and the time 100 nanoseconds; but the distance could as well have been billions of light years and the time billions of years. Thus the observing equipment in the here and the now, according to our last-minute decision whether to put in the second half-silvered mirror or take it out, has an irretrievable consequence for what we have the right to say about a photon that was given out long before there was any life in the universe.

We do not have to imagine all the equipment for this doing of a delayed-choice split-beam experiment at the cosmological scale. A split-beam is already in hand, fascinating discovery of the astrophysics of 1979.

Among quasars, those distant lighthouses of the universe which put out one hundred times as much light as our Milky Way or any other normal galaxy, is one that appears double (Figure 4). All available evidence goes to indicate that this doubling comes about much as does the double image of a street light as viewed through the distorting effect of a bubble in the window glass. About a quarter of the way from us to a

---

Figure 4. The double quasi-stellar object ("quasar": red shift $z = 1.41$), identified by its right ascension and declination as 0957 + 561 A, B, and believed to be the two images—produced by "gravitational lens action" of one and the same quasar. The intervening galaxy, and cluster of galaxies, responsible for this gravitational lens action (red shift $z = 0.39$) are fainter than the more distant but more brilliant quasar and therefore do not show on this photograph. (The photograph was made at the University of Hawaii telescope by Alan Stockton and was kindly communicated and discussed by Derek Wills of the University of Texas at Austin. It is the digital sum of five one-minute exposures in red light. The images appear elongated because of a telescope tracking problem.)

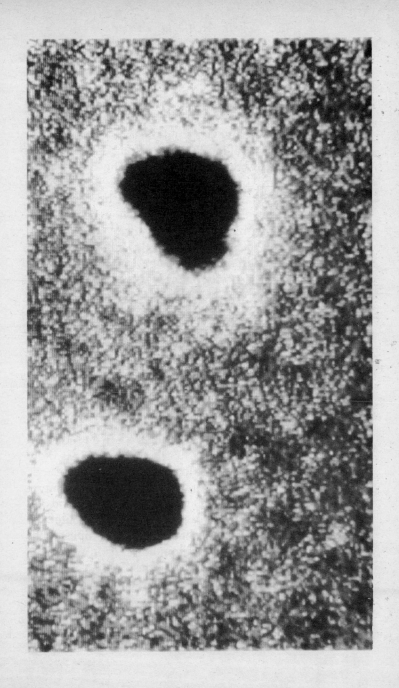

distant quasar is an intervening galaxy and cluster of galaxies. Its gravitational action, so the evidence indicates, is enough to take two light waves spread apart by 50,000 light years on their way out from the emitting atom on the quasar, and bring them back together at the earth. That is the explanation of the double image of a single quasar.

Two tracks, each 5 billion light years long, cannot be expected to be exactly identical in length. The difference is estimated to be perhaps of the order of magnitude of a month. Every electrical engineer of our day knows how to build a "delay line" which will delay a signal long enough for another signal to catch up with it. Nothing in principle prevents one imagining such a delay circuit sufficiently far beyond present capability that it will hold up the signal arriving from the quasar on the slightly shorter track long enough so that it will enter the telescope in perfect timing with the signal traveling the longer route from the same quasar.

Nothing prevents our bringing together the synchronized waves arriving by the two routes by a half-silvered mirror according to the plan illustrated on the righthand side of Figure 2. Then the counter in front will be clicking away all the time. The counter in back will never go off. In this way we will have evidence, to use again a mistaken way of speaking, that each photon came to us from the atom on the quasar "by both routes"—even though those routes are five billion light years long and separated from each other by 50,000 light years as they pass on the two sides of the intervening galaxy!

Alternatively, as in the laboratory experiment, we can remove that half-silvered mirror at the last minute and find out, again in a mistaken way of speaking, by "which route" the photon came. But the photon had already accomplished its travel before we made our last-minute decision whether it should travel "one route" or "both routes"!

We see here, more dramatically than in any example one can easily give, the difficulties of speaking of what goes on in the old-fashioned language of determinism. What a difficulty for Einstein! What a difficulty for the view that all that is and was exists "out there," independent of the choices made by the community of observers in the here and now! We grasp with renewed clarity the central lesson of the quantum, "No elementary quantum phenomenon is a phenomenon until it is a registered phenomenon."

Phenomenon and the Building of All That Is

The phenomenon we are dealing with in the proposed "double-quasar experiment" is spread out over billions of light years of space and billions of years of time. It is defined in part by the atom on the distant quasar. But it is also defined by the observer's decision whether to put the half-silvered mirror in or to take it out. It is intangible. It cannot be taken apart. It is not a particle. It is not a field of force. It is not spacetime. More ethereal than any of those older candidates for the building material of all that is, it is also altogether deprived of any of their internal structure.

How did the universe come into being? Is that some strange, far-off process beyond hope of analysis? Or is the mechanism that comes into play one which all the time shows itself (Figure 5)? Of all the signs that testify to "quantum phenomenon" as being the elementary act and building block of existence, none is more striking than its utter absence of internal structure and its untouchability. For a process of creation that can and does operate anywhere, that is more basic than particles or fields or spacetime geometry themselves, a process that reveals and yet hides itself, what could one have dreamed up out of pure imagination more magic and more fitting than this?

Observer as Participator

We used to think of the universe as "out there," to be observed as it were from behind the screen of a foot-thick slab plate of glass, safely, without personal involvement. The truth, quantum theory tells us, is quite different. Even when

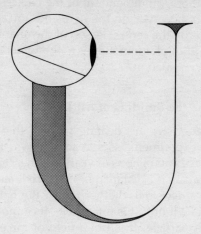

Figure 5. The Universe viewed as a "self-excited circuit." The universe, symbolized by the letter U, starts small at the big bang (upper right), grows in size, gives rise to life and observers and observing equipment; and the observing equipment, in turn, through the elementary quantum processes that terminate on it, takes part in giving a tangible "reality" to events that occurred long before there was any life anywhere.

we want to observe, not a galaxy, not a star, but something so miniscule as an electron, we have, in effect, to smash the glass, to reach in, and install measuring equipment. Bohr's principle of complementarity, Heisenberg's principle of indeterminism, and the lesson of "phenomenon" tell us more. We can install a device to measure the position, x, of the electron, or one to measure its momentum, p, but we can't fit both registering devices into the same place at the same time. Moreover, the act of registration has an inescapable consequence for what we have the right to say about the electron then and in the future. The observer is inescapably promoted to participator (Figure 6). In some strange sense, this is a participatory universe.

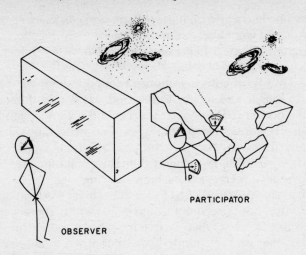

Figure 6. "Observer" promoted to "participator."

The Surprise Version of the Game of Twenty Questions

What is the difference between a "participatory" reality and a reality that exists "out there" independent of the community of perceivers? An example may illustrate a little of the difference. Edward Teller and I, and a dozen other guests, were sitting in the living room of Lothar Nordheim in Durham after dinner. From general conversation we moved on to the game of twenty questions. One, chosen as victim, was sent out of the room. The rest of us agreed on some implausible word like "brontosaurus." Then the victim was let back into the room. To win, he had to discover the word with no more than twenty yes/no questions. Otherwise, he lost.

After we had played several rounds, my turn came and I was sent out. The door was closed, and was kept closed for the longest time. I couldn't understand at all why they were taking so long. Moreover, when at length they let me in, every one had a grin on his face, sure sign of a joke or a trick. However, I went ahead innocently asking my questions. "Is it animal?" "No." "Is it vegetable?" "No." "Is it mineral?" "Yes." "Is it green?" "No." "Is it white?" "Yes."

As I went on with my queries I found the answerer was taking longer and longer to respond. He would think and think and think. Why? That was beyond my understanding when all I wanted was a simple yes or no answer. But finally, I knew, I had to chance it, propose a definite word. "Is it 'cloud'?" I asked. My friend thought a minute. "Yes," he said, finally. Then everyone burst out laughing.

My colleagues explained to me that when I was sent out of the room, they agreed not to agree on a word. There was no word in the room when I came in! What is more, they had agreed that each respondent was permitted to answer my question as he pleased—with one small proviso: if I challenged him, he had to have in mind a word compatible with his own and all the previous answers! The game, in other words, was just as difficult for my colleagues as for me.

What is the symbolism of the story? The world, we once believed, exists "out there," independent of any act of observation. The electron in the atom we once considered to have at each moment a definite position and a definite momentum. I, entering, thought the room contained a definite word. In actuality the word was developed step by step through the questions I raised, as the information about the electron is brought into being by the experiment that the observer chooses to make; that is, by the kind of registering equipment that he puts into place. Had I asked different questions or the same questions in a different order I would have ended up with a different word as the experimenter would have ended up with a different story for the doings of the electron. However, the power I had in bringing the particular word "cloud" into being was partial only. A major part of the selection lay in the "yes" and "no" replies of the colleagues around the room. Similarly, the experimenter has some substantial influence on what will happen to the electron by the choice of experiments he will do on it, "questions he will put to nature"; but he knows there is a certain unpredictability about what any given one of his measurements will disclose, about what "answers nature will give," about what will happen when "God plays dice." This comparison between the world of quantum observations and the surprise version of the game of twenty questions misses much, but it makes the central point. In the game, no word is a word until that word is promoted to reality by the choice of questions asked and answers given. In the real world of quantum physics, *no elementary phenomenon is a phenomenon until it is a recorded phenomenon*.

It is difficult to escape asking a challenging question. Is the entirety of existence, rather than being built on particles or fields of force or multidimensional geometry, built upon billions upon billions of elementary quantum phenomena, those elementary acts of "observer-participancy," those most ethereal of all the entities that have been forced upon us by the progress of science?

At first sight no question could seem more ridiculous. How fantastic the disproportion seems between the microscopic scale of the typical quantum phenomenon and the gigantic reach of the universe! Disproportion, however, we have learned, does not give us the right to dismiss. Else how would we have discovered that the heat of the carload of molten pig iron goes back for its explanation to the random motions of billions of microscopic atoms and the shape of the elephant to the message on a microscopic strand of DNA? Is the term "big bang" merely a shorthand way to describe the cumulative consequence of billions upon billions of elementary acts of observer-participancy reaching back into the past?

Stepping stone though this question may be to a new outlook, it is beset before and beyond by traps. One trap is a misjudgment of the role of "consciousness." The other is an exaggerated estimate of the category of "time."

Consciousness, we have been forced to recognize, has nothing whatsoever to do with the quantum process. We are dealing with an event that makes itself known by an irreversible act of amplification, by an indelible record, an act of registration. Does that record subsequently enter into the consciousness of some person, some animal or some computer? Is that the first step in translating the measurement into "meaning"—meaning regarded as "the joint product of all the evidence that is available to those who communicate"? Then that is a separate part of the story, important but not to be confused with "quantum phenomenon."

"Time" we too easily view as a pre-established umbrella, stretching over the scene of physics from big bang to gravitational collapse and beyond, extending from everlasting to everlasting. We once likewise thought of elasticity as a primordial concept. Today, we know that elasticity, however useful in describing the properties of a sheet of glass or a sheet of rubber, makes no sense in the space between the atomic electron and the nucleus. Out of the quantum theory of the motion of the electron, we construct elasticity as a secondary and derived concept. Likewise, in time to come, we will surely understand "time" as a term that makes no sense at all under extreme conditions and that derives its meaning under everyday conditions from a line of reasoning that makes no reference at all to time in the first place. In making progress in this direction, we have Gottfried Leibniz to inspire us, who stated in his great debate with Isaac Newton that "Time and space are not things but orders of things," and Einstein, who in his day reminded us, "Time and space are modes by which we think and not conditions in which we live."

Guided by these warnings and encouraged by the view that there is nothing at all of physics more elementary than "elementary quantum phenomena," are we destined some coming century to see all of existence derived out of this utterly primitive unit? And on the way, are we not surely destined to find some single simple idea that will lend itself to statement in a single sentence, so compelling that we will all say to one another, "Oh, how simple!" and "How stupid we all were!" and "How could it have been otherwise?"

Have I been making the world sound like a very mysterious place? It is! But amid all mysteries, we remember those great words of Leibniz, "Although the whole of this life were said to be nothing but a dream and the physical world nothing but a phantasm, I should call this dream or phantasm real enough, if, using reason well, we were never deceived by it."

There are many sources of energy. There is solar energy and the energy of fossil fuels, coal and oil. There is the energy of uranium, but a source of energy greater than any of these is the energy of the human heart, the energy that makes us reach for an understanding of the universe and our place in it, our responsibilities, our opportunities, our hopes. No questions are more pertinent to this comprehension than "How did the world come into being?" and "How is the world constructed?" I know of no clue more likely to allow us someday to grasp an understanding of these questions than the quantum.

Einstein, at the end of his book *Essays in Science,* wrote, "All of these endeavors are based on the belief that existence should have a completely harmonious structure. Today we have less ground than ever before for allowing ourselves to be forced away from this wonderful belief."

WHEELER: *Conversations*

ELVEE: Dr. Wheeler, who was there to observe the universe when it started? Were we there? Or does it only start with our observation? Is the big bang here?

WHEELER: A lovely way to put it—"Is the big bang here?" I can imagine that we will someday have to answer your question with a "yes." If there is any conclusion that follows more strongly than another about the nature of time from the study of the quantum nature of space and time, it is the circumstance that the very idea of "before" and "after" is in some sense transcended.

There are two aspects of this idea. First, Einstein's theory of space and time tells us that in order to predict all of space and time for time to come, we have to know what the conditions of space are now and how fast they're changing. Only then do we have enough information to predict all the future. The uncertainty principle of quantum theory tells us that if we know the condition of space now, we cannot know how fast it's changing. Or if we know how fast it's changing now, we cannot know what the geometry is now. Nature is so built with this complementary feature that we cannot have the information we need to give a deterministic account of space geometry evolving with time.

That deterministic account of space evolving in time is what we mean by spacetime. Everything that we say in everyday language about time is directly built on that concept. And with determinism out, the very ideas of before and after are also out. For practical everyday matters, this indeterminism, this indefinability of space-time is of no concern. The uncertainties only show up effectively at distances of the order of 10^{-33} cm. Nobody at present has equipment fine enough to reach down to a distance so small.

What does all this have to do with the big bang? At the very beginning of time we know that—according to Einstein's account —the universe was indefinitely small. Things were indefinitely compact. When we talk about time when the universe itself is so fantastically small, we deal with a state of affairs where the very words "before" and "after" lose all meaning. This circumstance puts one heavy restriction on the usefulness of the word "time." There is another.

When we do our observations in the here and the now on photons, quanta of light, hunks of energy coming from distant astrophysical sources, we ourselves have an irretrievable part in bringing about that which appears to be happening. We can put it this way: that reality is, in a certain sense, made up of a few iron posts of definite observation between which we fill in, by an elaborate work of imagination and theory, all the rest of the construction that we call reality. In other words, we are wrong to think of the past as having a definite existence "out there." The past only exists insofar as it is present in the records of today. And what those records are is determined by what questions we ask. There is no other history than that. This is the sense in which we ourselves are involved in defining the conditions of individual elementary quantum phenomena way back at the beginning of the big bang.

Each elementary quantum phenomenon is an elementary act of "fact creation." That is incontestable. But is that the *only* mechanism needed to create all that is? Is what took place at the big bang the

consequence of billions upon billions of these elementary processes, these elementary "acts of observer-participancy," these quantum phenomena? Have we had the mechanism of creation before
our eyes all this time without recognizing the truth? That is the
larger question implicit in your comment. Of all the deep questions of our time, I do not know one that is deeper, more exciting,
more clearly pregnant with a great advance in our understanding.

RORTY: What puzzles me is the degree to which the surprisingness
of quantum physics is an empirical, and the degree to which it is a
philosophical matter. That is, what I don't know enough to grasp
is whether the philosophical overlay on science, the nineteenth-
century philosophical account of the nature of science, was so
inadequate in itself that practically *anything* would make one doubt
it. As it happened, quantum phenomena did. But it may have
been so faked up that it merely needed a suggestion to collapse in
favor of something like a pragmatist understanding of science. But
I take it that Professor Wheeler feels that it is quite specific quantum
results that simply contradict fundamental empirical theses which
had been presupposed by the older theories. So the relation is
much more direct.

WHEELER: Heisenberg, on his last visit to this country, staying at
our house, was telling me at breakfast about a discussion that took
place on board the sailboat between Sweden and Denmark shortly
after he had sent in his paper for publication on the uncertainty
principle. And in that discussion on board the sailboat [between]
Niels Bohr, Niels Bjerrum, the great chemist, and Heisenberg,
Bjerrum was asking Heisenberg to tell him about it, and he went
on for quite some length. When he had finished, the chemist,
Niels Bjerrum, turned to Niels Bohr and said, "But Niels, that's all
what you've been telling me ever since you were a student at the
University," as if somehow it was not the quantum theory that had
led to complementarity, but complementarity had already existed
in his thinking. And as Flexner always put it, "chance favors the
prepared mind." Here was a mind that was prepared to capitalize
on this feature of nature and exploit it, recognize it. I think it would
be fair to say that he did not impose his own philosophical outlook
on nature. I don't know anybody who has any doubt about the
uncertainty principle in the larger world of science. I don't know
anybody who has any doubt that you can study one aspect of
nature and know one aspect, but it keeps you from knowing the
other. Nature is so built that you cannot know both. I don't know

anybody who thinks that that was an epistemology that came from philosophy, but was not right there, driven on by the very formalism itself. And, of course, it's been one of the great miracles of physics, how the equations themselves, at every step of the way, have been our surest guide in learning what the right interpretation is.

WIGNER: I think it may be good if something very down to earth, and very unpleasant, is added to what Professor Wheeler has said. This is that most of us believe that quantum mechanics is not really consistent with all phenomena. This was overtly implied by Professor Wheeler when he suggested that even though for atoms and molecules, and perhaps many other things, quantum mechanics is valid, for us it is not valid. The process of observation cannot be described by quantum mechanics. It leads to a very, very definite contradiction. Where this lack of validity of quantum mechanics enters, we don't really know.

Until about three years ago, I thought that it is life which is not contained in quantum mechanics . . . the existence of a consciousness. In fact, quantum mechanics can be formulated, not very nicely, but very truly, by saying that it gives probability connections between subsequent observations. But it does not describe the observations. However, what I thought is not really valid. As Professor Wheeler already indicated, sometimes an experiment, a measurement, or an observation is finished when the light strikes a photographic plate and darkens it. This is really a surprise. Most of us believed and, to some degree, I still believe that the darkening of the photographic plate can still be described by quantum mechanics and that it is neither dark nor not dark, as it would follow from the quantum mechanical equations that it is in a *super position* of darkness and not darkness. And this, of course, indicates that we should extend science or physics, or whatever it is, further, so that it encompasses this transition between microscopic and macroscopic. But as the silver chloride or silver bromide of the photographic plate is microscopic or macroscopic is not clear, but this is what we should try to understand. I hope you will contradict me.

WHEELER: Professor Wigner and I have been discussing together for years, and I always learn so much new. But on this issue also we share the concern about how one can talk of an irreversible act of amplification, as what it is that brings a phenomenon to a close, that defines it. And Eugene Wigner then asks, "What means irreversible?" And there always comes the stage where, if we use the mathematical machinery, the mathematical machinery doesn't say, "Well, here's the moment where it's been observed." You never get to that point. You go from the pupil to the retina, from the retina to the brain, and so on. It's very related to Professor Rorty's comment that we're dealing with a pragmatic description and from the pragmatic point of view we say, "Well, there it is. It's happened." And that's it. But a person of real conscience, like Professor Wigner, says, "Let's understand it" and we bow down and say, "Well, we agree," we haven't seen all the details pieced out with the help of our present day mathematical machinery.

WIGNER: Perhaps I should make my point even a little clearer than Professor Wheeler has made it. Namely, that there is evidently or apparently a transition between microscopic and macroscopic. Quantum mechanics deals with microscopic phenomena, which it describes validly. But they are reversible. They are reversible. Macroscopic phenomena are, as he pointed out, not reversible. If I have seen something I have seen it and that is the end of it, and I am not in what quantum mechanics calls in a super position of having seen it, or not having seen it, so that my state can be reversed, so that I have done neither.

WHEELER: You can't unforget.

WIGNER: I can't unremember. I can forget, and I am good at it. Not in every case. And I think this transition between microscopic and macroscopic is not contained in present day physics. And we should strive in that direction. Perhaps I will say, in a very boasting way, that I am proposing an equation for that, which is not yet in print. But it is that our behavior is such as Einstein imagined it, that there are real facts, and he even imagined that there are world lines in spacetime. And that those really do exist, but quantum mechanics contradicts that. But where is the transition between the existence of reality and the existence of a quantum description, which does not contain reality in the everyday sense, but gives only probabilities for things or something of that sort. That is not clear now and I think it would be wonderful to investigate it. And perhaps if we understand it we will come closer to the problem of the mind.

GRANIT: Well, I'd like to stick my head into this discussion. Of course, it is the head of the *advocatus diaboli*. As we have developed in humanity this tremendous scientific apparatus, it has been accomplished by the fragmentation of knowledge. So I raise the question. Who really believes that this is the only road to the knowledge of natural phenomena, fragmentation to the last bits, so that finally you are in this conflicting situation of not being able to observe whether light is a wave or a particle, without two operations which can't simultaneously be observed. But it seems to me that complementarity is such a general notion that it is almost without value. We can speak about mind and about the material as also complementarily organized. We can speak of hundreds of things as being complementary one to the other. I think complementarity gives you very little to hang on to.

WHEELER: It's certainly true that Niels Bohr ran into more and more flak, the wider the realm of discourse to which he applied the concept of complementarity. For example, he thought of using it in connection with the old issue about free will versus determinism. They seem like complementary concepts. Bohr with his order of nobility, for which he had the symbol of the Yin-Yang, also supplied some Latin words and the words he chose were "non contraria, sed complementa." And to him there was no contradiction between free will and determinism because what free will means is the opportunity of a person to decide as he will what he will do. And what does determinism mean? It means that if you could take apart the brain of that person and measure all the electrochemical potentials and everything else, then you could predict exactly what would happen next. Well, of course, if you thought of doing that you would, by that very token, destroy the very life of the person. There would be no opportunity to exercise free will, and so the two points of view are not complementary. You can use one or the other, but you can't use both at the same time for the same person. This was not welcomed by everybody and it's true that there's no equation associated with this idea and physicists are regarded as trespassing if they deal with the realm where they can't give an equation.

WIGNER: I would go further, Professor, if you forgive me, I would go further. Even if you measure everything in the brain you should, according to quantum mechanics, not measure potentials but obtain the wave function . . . the state vector. And the state vector will not tell you, really, whether he will go to the left or go to the right, because it may be in a superposition of the two. And this shows more clearly again what I'm trying to say. That, for macroscopic phenomena, quantum mechanics in its present form is not yet applicable.

PANNENBERG: I felt that Professor Wheeler quite intentionally created bewilderment in his audience this morning, by leaving the impression that the mind is everything. And the bewilderment of course was that it is hard to believe that a scientist would sacrifice the claim to objectivity in his science. And so there was a tension emerging. It is so difficult, in our tradition, to avoid an alternative; either what is conceived by human knowledge is taken as something quite independent from being known, or it is considered to be merely subjective. I take it you have a position in between and do not accept this alternative.

I think that we have a similar situation in the historical disciplines. Collingwood, in his book on the idea of history, made the point very brilliantly that we can have no historical data without interpretation. And even the evidence we call upon to control the interpretation of historians is again evidence only in a particular interpretation which makes it the evidence. On the other hand, historical interpretation is not completely arbitrary either. Would you say there is a parallel to your thought in this historical interpretation? Or do you want to say something different from that?

WHEELER: Of course, we can go back already to the days of Vico, who reminds us as a historian that we're involved in creating what we call historical proof. I like the story of the three baseball umpires relaxing over beer one afternoon and comparing notes. One umpire says, "I calls 'em as I sees 'em." The next umpire says, "I calls 'em as they really are." The third one says, "They ain't nothin' until I calls 'em." This point of history being made in the act of making decisions is relevant to the historical context.

PANNENBERG: You didn't say much on the field concept in your description of content. Could you comment a little on the potential of field theory to include the element of chance?

WHEELER: The concept, of course, of something like the electromagnetic field pervading all space or space itself, its dynamics, the curvatures of space, as they show up in gravitation, constituting a field. Or, in our own day, more extensive fields which are spread out. It's true that they fall under the domain of quantum theory. They are more complex than the notion of a particle in the sense that they are endowed with infinite numbers of degrees of freedom, which introduces problems of its own. And those problems are important. But the real issues about quantum theory somehow seem to encompass both fields and particles. So, in this sense, I'm not sure that there is any new critical appraisal of quantum theory that comes in from the fields. Except for the fact that it's difficult to see how to reconcile a quantum theoretical account with an account of phenomena propagated in space and time. This is one of the central issues of our day: how to comprise relativity and quantum theory in a larger unity.

The Place of Mind in Nature*

KARL POPPER

The topic on which I am to speak was not my choice: it was chosen by the organizers of this conference. It was an ambitious choice, and I was, at first, shocked: I certainly would not have dared to choose such a theme myself. But after thinking it over for a time I was glad to have been given this task which is so obviously beyond my powers, and which I should never have dared to choose myself.

I

Let me therefore say at once, as an introduction, that I am fully aware of my limitations, and of my incompetence. I know how little I know; and even this I have not discovered: I have learned it from someone else—from Socrates. Thus all the things I am going to say in this lecture are to be taken as suggestions; at best, as conjectures. And at the very best, there may be, perhaps, here or there, a testable conjecture.

I say "at the very best" because a testable and well-tested conjecture is, I suggest, the very best kind of knowledge we can have. Thus, I suggest, even our best knowledge is tentative knowledge, conjectural knowledge. This includes the natural sciences: even scientific knowledge remains conjectural, although it is the best knowledge we have. It is tenta-

---

* Owing to illness, the author was unable to deliver this lecture.

tive knowledge that has been severely criticized. It consists of testable, tentative conjectures.

We cannot reach certainty: not even the best theories of the natural sciences are certain. (They cannot even be said to be more probable than improbable, if we take probability in any of the senses that satisfy the laws of the calculus of probability.[1]) All we can do is to criticize them, and to test them, as severely as our ingenuity permits.

II

This view of mine has often been misunderstood. Thus it has often been said, wrongly, that I reject the concept of truth. I do not: I think that truth is the aim of all our intellectual endeavors.

A statement or a proposition or a conjecture or a theory is true if, and only if, it agrees with (or corresponds to) the facts. Indeed, everybody knows this: if, in a court of law, you are reminded that you should speak the truth, you know very well that you are supposed to say what agrees with the facts.[2] It is clear that you can only do your best and say what you subjectively believe to be true. Yet you (and the judge) will know that the truth is objective, and that, as we are fallible, it is human to err, to make a mistake: to believe subjectively what is not the objective truth. The idea of fallibility involves the idea of an objective truth, a truth from which we may stray, err, deviate.

Thus truth is objective; also, it is not relative to a language, but absolute. The highly improbable possibility has to be admitted that the same sequence of noises which expresses a true statement in the English language may happen to express a false statement in the French language or in the Chinese language. But this does not mean (as has been asserted) that truth is relative to the language. On the contrary, if an unambiguous statement is true in English, then all its translations (in all those languages into which it can be translated) will also be true; and if it is false in English, then all its translations will also be false. Thus truth and falsity are not only objective, but they are absolute.[3]

The claim that truth is objective and absolute may sound arrogant; and it would be arrogant if it were combined with the claim that we know the truth; or that we possess a criterion of truth, that is to say, some means by which we can recognize a proposition that agrees with the facts. But to say that truth is objective and absolute is far from arrogant when it is combined with fallibilism, with the doctrine that the possibility of error affects all, or almost all, our knowledge, and that it makes all our best and most interesting knowledge conjectural.

This fallibilism was first formulated by the Greek pre-Socratic philosopher Xenophanes, born (it is thought) in 571 before Christ, in the Ionian city of Colophon. He formulated his philosophy in verses, and some fragments of it have been preserved. I give here my translation of one of these fragments which contains his theory of truth, of fallibilism, and of conjectural knowledge:

> But as for certain truth, no man has known it,
> Nor will he know it; neither of the gods,
> Nor yet of all the things of which I speak.
> And even if by chance he were to utter
> The perfect truth, he would himself not know it.
> For all is but a woven web of guesses.[4]

In these verses Xenophanes teaches the fallibility of human knowledge. But the verses contain more: they say that even our most perfect knowledge is conjectural: it is "a woven web of guesses." And they contain (if only implicitly and perhaps almost unconsciously) a theory of objective truth. For they say clearly that something I utter may be a perfect and true description of the facts—yet it may be so by chance, without my being aware of the fact that it is true. Thus truth is objective, independent of anybody's personal knowledge.

Truth is simply the agreement with the facts of what has been said, whether or not anybody is aware of that agreement.

Yet the lines of Xenophanes which I have quoted entail something beyond this. They say, as we have seen, that *truth* can never be known with *certainty;* and this means that we have to distinguish sharply between truth and certainty: truth is objective, and may be achieved. Certainty, or certain truth, cannot be achieved at all. Thus the distinction between truth and certainty is of decisive importance.

In all this I agree with Xenophanes.

Even our best knowledge, the well-tested scientific knowledge of the physical and biological sciences, is fallible: it is *conjectural knowledge.* But what I am now going to present to you in this lecture is, I fear, mostly far from scientific knowledge. It consists of the suggestions of a mere amateur, of one who merely loves and admires science as one of the greatest, most daring, and most beautiful adventures of the human mind in its search for truth.

III

With this I have arrived at the human mind, and at one of *the* most important products of its search for truth: natural science.

It certainly is the most progressive one. In science we have real progress. A new theory is tentatively accepted by physicists or biologists only if they have reason to think that it is better than its predecessor: if it has greater explanatory power, and if it is better testable. Of course, the scientists may be mistaken in their judgment. But the question is an objective one, and usually they are right, at least in the long run.

Thus science evolves; and since there is a feedback between the human mind and its products, such as science, the human mind evolves too.

Not only do we have new material tools as the result of progress in the physical and biological sciences, but we have also new mental tools, new and better ways of asking questions, new and better ways of seeking answers, new and better ways of calculating and preventing unwanted consequences of our actions. All these are purely mental achievements; and thus we can say that the human mind evolves.

IV

For such reasons, I may call myself an evolutionist, first of all with respect to the human mind. But I am also an evolutionist with respect to the rest of nature: with respect to life on earth, and with respect to the universe.

In saying that I am an evolutionist I do not, of course, wish to say more than that I accept, very tentatively, the current theories of the evolution of the stars and of life on earth. The reason for tentatively accepting these theories is their immense explanatory power. I am also an ardent admirer of Darwinism; of Mendelianism; and of their synthesis ("The Modern Synthesis" as Julian Huxley called it). Yet, at the same time, I regard it as a matter of course that we have to try to adopt a highly critical attitude especially towards those theories which we admire most; such as Darwinism, that is, the theory of natural selection, supported by modern genetics —the theory of heredity that grew out of Mendelianism.

V

What is the central problem of Darwinism? What does natural selection explain? According to Darwin, it explains the origin of the different species of plants and animals; and by this Darwin means the design, the well-adapted structures, of the millions of different species of organisms that inhabit the earth.

I distinguish between three fairly different problems faced by Darwinism:

1. The problem of the origin of species in the sense of the

splitting up of a species into two or more species (or the problem of the division of one gene pool into two or more). This problem needs for its solution some auxiliary theory, such as geographic isolation.

2. The problem of the immense variety of living species. This problem also needs for its solution some auxiliary theory, such as a theory that explains the invasion of life into many different and changing environments.

3. The problem of adaptation—of the complexity of organisms and their functions, and of the marvelous adaptability of these functions to each other and to the environment. This seems to be the central problem for Darwin; and his answer to it was: natural selection.

(To these three main problems we may perhaps add a fourth: the problem of overspecialization and the consequent extinction of species.)

I believe that the central problem for Darwin was, in spite of the title of his book, the problem of adaptation or, in other words, the problem of the wonderful design of organisms. It is explained in Darwinism by the theory of evolutionary change and by natural selection.

The theory of evolution explains adaptation as the result of a history of many steps of small improvements—just as, say, the design of our bicycles or motor cars or typewriters or watches can be explained as a result of many steps of (comparatively) small improvements. And the analogy with the improvements of our machines can be carried a little further. In improving machines, we operate largely by trial and the elimination of error. We look out for parts that do not work too well, and we think of possible variants: these are our trials. And we eliminate those variants which in their turn do not work too well: this is the elimination of our errors. In the case of the organism, the variants, called the mutations, are not planned. They are the results of random errors of the hereditary copying mechanism. What is copied are the genes, and the mutations which are the results of copying errors enrich the gene pool, and so the available variants within a species. This corresponds to the trials in our attempts to improve our machines.

To our rejection or elimination of the bad (or erroneous) trials, in the case of our machines, corresponds the action of the environmental conditions which reduce the frequency of the unfavorable mutations by killing their carriers, while those mutations which are favorable because their carriers become well-adapted individuals will spread in the population.

VI

According to this theory, the element of novelty enters the design of organisms only through mutations; and as mutations are random, as they are chance mistakes of the copying mechanism that controls heredity, the novelty is the result of pure chance. On the other hand, all that is not chance—all adaptation, all improvement, all design—is entirely the result of the killing powers of the environment of the organisms —of a hostile environment that includes predators (such as bacteria) and also the competitors of the same species. This killing power of the environment is usually called "selection pressure." The selection pressure of natural selection thus does all the designing; it does it by killing, by cutting away those mutations that are not wanted, because they are not adapted—somewhat like a sculptor who cuts away the marble or the wood that is not wanted. Thus, according to this interpretation of the theory of natural selection, all the designing power lies in the selection pressure of the hostile environment. The evolving organism does not, in its turn, contribute, except by passively producing mutations: chance mistakes of the hereditary copying mechanism.[5]

I shall call the version of Darwinism just described "the theory of the hostile environment" or, briefly, "passive Darwinism." (There is even a theory that I am inclined to call "tough Darwinism." It is the combination of passive Darwinism and determinism. Passive Darwinism as such can admit indeterminism, for example, by pointing out that mutations are often the results of chance; for instance of radiation which, in its turn, is the result of quantum jumps.)

One of the main characteristics of what I call passive Darwinism is this. A passive Darwinist holds that the mindlike properties of an organism, such as alertness, curiosity, or the preference for certain kinds of food, play a role in evolution exactly like its bodily properties such as size or color of the hair or the eyes. Both kinds of properties are to be regarded as the "expressions" of the genes (the genotype, the genome) of the organism, and as more or less successful adaptations to the environment, and as well-fitting or ill-fitting certain possible changes of the environment. The preferences or "aims" of the organism, more particularly, do not play any special role in the theoretical explanation of what happens in evolution. As one great evolutionist formulated it in 1959, the modern theory "can be characterised by two postulates: (1) that all the events that lead to the production of new genotypes . . . are essentially random and not in any way finalistic [that is, related to the "aims" of the organism]; and (2) that the order . . . in the . . . adaptations . . . is due to . . . natural selection."[6]

There is little doubt that passive Darwinism is a theory of great explanatory power, and that it brilliantly explains, for example, what biologists call "industrial melanism"—the replacement of light-colored moths by dark colored ones. The trunks of certain light-colored trees in the United Kingdom are blackened by industrial smoke. Dark-colored forms of moths can conceal themselves against this dark background, while the light-colored moths (originally the vast majority) are now very visible and fall prey to their enemies. Thus they are eliminated by natural selection, because they are no longer well-adapted in this changed environment. But the previously rare dark variants survive, and now form the majority.

There are several examples of this kind. A very famous and important case is that of strains of mosquitoes that have become resistant to a particular kind of insecticide (such as

DDT) that has been applied on a massive scale; or the case of strains of bacteria that have become resistant to penicillin or other antibiotics. In all these examples it seems that some rare gene (or genes) existed in the gene pool *before* the environment changed and became more hostile and thus more selective, and that this originally rare gene turned out to make its carrier well-adapted to the changed environment.

These examples show very clearly that passive Darwinism works. It does so, at least, in many cases. But more can be said: although passive Darwinism is, of course, no more than a conjecture, I do not wish to deny the possibility (assuming that it includes the theories of genetic drift and of geographic isolation) that passive Darwinism may be *the* true and sufficient explanatory theory of the evolution of life on earth. Nevertheless, I conjecture that it is not sufficient.

My conjecture is that we must add to what I call the theory of the hostile environment or passive Darwinism a second and complementary theory which I call the theory of the friendly environment, or exploratory Darwinism, or active Darwinism.

VII

The theory which I call exploratory or active Darwinism does not go beyond Darwinism; it merely assumes that, very early in the history of life on earth, living organisms acquired, presumably by way of mutations organized by selection pressure, certain behavioral traits: they became active explorers, actively and curiously searching for new environments—for what biologists call new ecological niches, that is, for new places to live in or, sometimes, merely for slightly modified ways of living, for slightly new ways of behaving, and especially for trial behavior.

But trial behavior implies that there are alternative ways of behavior—a behavioral repertoire; and that there are evaluations: the organism must find out whether one of the available types of behavior is more successful than another type.

Presumably, this implies, in its turn, that the behavior can lead to something like pain or to pleasure, and that it is changed if it leads to pain.

If we assume that such active and exploratory and mindlike (and presumably partly conscious) behavior is the result of the very early evolution brought about by passively Darwinian forces, then we can also assume that, once this stage has been reached, evolution is no longer the passive result of heredity and a hostile environment. Mindlike properties of the organism will begin to play an increasingly important part in evolution: aims, such as preference for certain kinds of mates, preferences for certain locations for breeding, or for certain types of food; but also curiosity and exploratory behavior and, by contrast, conservative behavior; or change from one kind of behavior to another. Such mindlike and actively Darwinian forces will become in time just as important as the passively Darwinian forces, and often more important.

Admittedly, a rigid determinist will see no difference between passive and active Darwinism; more precisely, all that I call "active Darwinism" he will reduce to, or explain within, passive Darwinism. For the determinist will hold that the aims or preferences and other mindlike behavioral trends of an organism are fully determined by its heredity and environment, so that they need not be specially mentioned in a causal analysis of the forces contributing to evolution. However, if only we admit that there are often probabilities (or propensities to act) rather than certainties determined by heredity in a given environmental situation, then the argument of the determinist collapses. And indeed, if we can learn anything from Mendelian genetics, we certainly should have learned one thing: the importance of probabilistic thinking, as opposed to rigid deterministic thinking.[7]

However, if we have probabilities or propensities for the genetic aspect, then nothing serious can be said against the reality (even the irreducible reality) or preferences of a mindlike character. And many competent biologists writing on evolution, especially on the evolution of birds, speak about the influence of psychological factors such as preferences.

But once we allow preferences to come in, we must allow that it is not only the hostile environment which plays an active, an organizing, a designing part in evolution, but also the active search of the organism for a preferred environment: for a friendly environment.

Passive Darwinism, I suggest, works mainly in such cases as the adaptation of bacteria to penicillin or of mosquitoes to DDT; that is to say, in cases of a more or less catastrophic change in the environment of the affected organism. These are changes which do not allow the organism to be active: either all members of the population are killed, or there are a few that are, by chance, well-adapted to the catastrophic change, and so survive.

But let us start with the case of a type of organism, or a genetic pool, that is reasonably well adapted to an environment that does not change in a catastrophic way. According to Darwin, the selection pressure will under such circumstances be due mainly to overpopulation: under such favorable conditions, the organism will multiply quickly, and if the environment, the ecological niche, the habitat, is limited—and our earth *is* limited—it will soon be too small, and its selection pressure, even upon a population well-adapted to the environment, will increase; that is to say, there will be an increased death rate. This, no doubt, will lead to a further rise of the standard of adaptation: the least adapted will, in the main, be killed. But with a high death rate, the most fertile will have the best chance of some of their offspring surviving, and we shall find, after some time, not so much an improvement in the adaptation to the external environment of this type of organism but a further adaptation to the internal selection pressures of overpopulation and the consequential high death rate; and this will be in the main a selection for high fertility.

This seems to me to be one of the real difficulties of passive Darwinism. But this problem may be soluble if we bring in active Darwinism; that is, something like mind. For in this case, we shall have mutations for exploratory behavior, for seeking other environments, new types of food, new ecological niches: a new habitat.

This is what biologists have seen and what they call *the habitat selection by the organism*. Of course, it can be conjectured that it has its basis in mutations, like everything else. But by actively selecting a new ecological niche, a new way of living, new preferences, a new habitat, the organism exposes itself to a new type of selection pressure, *a selection pressure that molds it to fit better into that new habitat, into that new way of life, which it has actively chosen, which it has preferred.*

In this way, the preference, the active choice made by the organism, turns into a choice of a characteristic kind of selection pressure, and in this way it can become the choice of a characteristic direction in the evolution of the species. Of course, if so, this is an unintended consequence of the habitat selection.

VIII

The history of this idea (sometimes called the "Baldwin effect") and its frequent rediscovery has been described by Sir Alister Hardy.[8] Hardy gives the following illustration:

> If birds of a particular species, originally feeding on insects from the surface of the bark of trees, found . . . that they could get more prey by probing into or under the bark, then they might develop a change of habit which, by being copied . . . could gradually spread . . . [by imitation. If] this new habit became well established, then any member of the population with a gene complex giving a break slightly better adapted to such probing would have a better chance of survival. . . .[9]

I myself had the same idea many years ago. I arrived at it in a slightly different way. I asked myself, What is likely to come first: a new preference or a new skill or a new change in the anatomy? In other words, a new way of behavior or a new bodily change? And I found that any new anatomic change would be a heavy burden, a disadvantage, if the organism does not functionally require it, or know how to use it: the new behavior and the need for the anatomic change must come first if the anatomic change is to be of any use to the organism. One might put it briefly: the mindlike requirement —the wish, the need, the preference—must change before the body.

I was very surprised to find that Darwin himself had considered the problem but had not seen its immense importance, and had, indeed, pushed it aside. He wrote:

> It would be easy for natural selection to adapt the structure of the animal to its changed habits.

However, he continued:

> It is . . . difficult to decide, and immaterial for us, whether habits generally change first, and structures afterwards, or whether slight modifications of structure lead to changed habits; both probably often occurring almost simultaneously. [10]

No doubt it is true that even a genetic mishap—a very unfavorable mutation, say—may cause a "habit," such as, for example, a limp. On the other hand, a new kind of animal behavior—what Darwin and even Sir Alister Hardy here describe as a new "habit"—may be much better described as a new invention; a new discovery; or even a newly discovered theory. And it may be the cause of an evolutionary breakthrough, as one can see from Alister Hardy's description.

Or take, as an example, the evolutionary emergence of limbs from fins. What is more likely: that the "habit" of *trying* to walk on the land—or, let us say it, the wish—came first, and the evolution of limbs came afterwards (of course, in many slow stages, and with feedback), or that it all started with an anatomical change of the fins? Of course, we do not know, and we shall never know: the question cannot be answered by science. Yet I regard it far more likely that a small change of "habit" produced a new kind of environment which in turn produced a new selection pressure which led to an anatomic change that was used at once because it suited the preferences or wishes of the animal, rather than that a small anatomic change occurred *and persisted unused* until some of the animals found out how it could be used, changing their preferences and "habits" accordingly.

I cannot stress sufficiently strongly that my hypothesis is not a scientific conjecture: since it cannot be tested, it should be described as a metaphysical conjecture. (The reason for its nontestability is that the two competing hypotheses do not so much describe observationally different events as different interpretations of sequences of events.) However, W. H. Thorpe has designed some beautiful experiments that induce artificially new behavioral preferences (such as preferred smells)[11]; experiments that seem to indicate that something similar to my hypothesis does sometimes happen. Of course, these experiments are not tests of my hypothesis: my hypothesis is, I repeat, untestable.

IX

I will now sum up my view of the prehistory of mind—of the prehistory of the human mind—in the evolution of animals, especially of the so-called higher animals. It is, in brief, this.

1. The beginnings of mindlike behavior can be found very early in evolution, perhaps as the result of passive Darwinism.

2. With the emergence of exploratory behavior, of tentative behavior, and of trial and error behavior, mindlike behavior plays an increasingly active part in evolution. This does not mean that Darwinian selection is transcended, but it means that active Darwinism (as I call it), the search for a friendly environment, the selection of a habitat by the organism, becomes important.

3. The relative importance of passive and active Darwinism in evolution can hardly be compared or weighed, just as one

cannot compare the relative importance of heredity and environment.

4. It seems that mindlike behavior turns into conscious behavior; at which stage we cannot say.

5. At any rate, it seems reasonable to assume, in spite of the metaphysical character of the assumption, that the human mind has an evolutionary prehistory: that the human mind evolves, that it can be regarded as a product of evolution; of an evolution in which the emerging mind plays a very active part.

6. Thus my thesis is that mind, prehuman and human takes a most active part in evolution and especially in its own evolution. We are largely active makers of ourselves; and our minds are largely makers of our place in nature.

X

Before turning from this conjectural survey of the part played by the prehuman mind in prehuman evolution to the tremendous role played by the human mind in the evolution of man, I wish to add a few remarks on what I regard as most characteristic of mind and of its exploring and experimenting predecessor.

1. I suggest that all organisms, plants as well as animals and humans, are problem solvers. They are constantly engaged, day and night, in solving many problems. Of course, they are unconscious problem solvers. Even humans are not always conscious of the problems they are trying to solve. (A typical such problem arises when we are just quietly standing upright. We are unaware that our nerves and muscles constantly "control" our posture, which they minutely "observe" and "correct".)

2. All these problems have a direction: they are all attempts to anticipate the future and to improve the prospects of the organism by anticipating future needs, or impending events. For this reason, they can be described as hypotheses or theories (or as primitive analogues to hypotheses or theories).

Many of these anticipations or expectations or hypotheses or theories are ways of behavior, especially tentative behavior (the trying out of a behavioral repertoire, or of a repertoire of preferences). And *vice versa:* many ways of behavior, especially exploratory behavior and mindlike behavior, amount to anticipations about the environment.

3. Thus, from a very early stage, problem solving and anticipations or theory construction about the environment play a central part in the behavior of organisms. They remain, I suggest, central throughout the whole range of higher organisms; especially, of course, of higher animals, including man.

XI

If we now look at the human mind from this point of view—as a problem solver, and as an evolutionary successor of problem solvers—then it seems that the most important event in the evolution of man and the human mind was one very specific step in the evolution of language: the great step from a signaling language, such as a language of warning cries—a language that releases certain reactions in another organism such as a flight—to a descriptive language: a language that can describe facts, after the fact has occurred, or before it has occurred.

It is of fundamental importance to be quite clear about these different uses of language.

Somebody tells me: "Stop the car. There is a tree across the road." These two sentences would seem to be typical of human language. But there is the language of the bees; and according to Karl von Frisch, the discoverer of the dancing language of the bees, a worker bee may tell its co-workers: "Fly in such a direction that the sun is 25 degrees to the right of your direction for 450 metres: there is some wonderful food waiting to be carried to the hive."

It must be admitted that of all animal languages of which we have any knowledge, the dancing language of the bee comes nearest to the human language. Bees can not only formulate advice for action, in connection with the search for food, or with the search for a new home, but they can also *describe*, by their dance, the position (relative to the hive and to the sun) of the object of interest, and characterize its quality. In this, they seem to go far beyond all other animals, although some birds not only utter warning cries ("Danger") but also seem to connect it with a rough *description* of the kind of danger ("fox!" or "hawk!" etc.).

XII

The great psychologist Karl Buhler, who was one of my teachers at the University of Vienna, distinguished three functions of language. The lowest of these three functions is the expressive function. It is always present when there is language, even if the organism that speaks happens to be alone and unobserved. It indicates the state of the speaking organism. In the case of the dancing bee, it could be translated as: "I am so excited about the nectar which I have found: I must dance." According to Buhler, we can also say that the linguistic behavior of the organism is a symptom or an expression of its inner state.

The second function of language according to Buhler is this: the linguistic behavior of the speaking organism releases in some other organism or organisms a reaction, a response. Thus these other organisms act as if they would interpret the behavior of the speaking organism as a stimulus, as a signal. Buhler calls this the release function, or the signal function. The dance of the bee functions from this point of view not only expressively ("I am excited by my encounter with the nectar!") but also as a signal, a command or advice ("Go and get the nectar"); and it is understood and taken up by the other bees.

This is, on the animal level, biologically the most important function.

Buhler's third function is the descriptive function. And by

this he means a function that transcends the animal languages, a function that is characteristic of the human language alone. He has in mind a description of an event that *may* not be connected with a warning or a command, a description whose main biological function may be to *convey information about some state of affairs*. This information may or may not be acted upon by the receiving organisms; and if acted upon, it may be acted upon in a situation unconnected with the situation in which the information was originally given.[12]

My own way of characterizing the descriptive function which, I think, Buhler had in mind is this: it arises when the information conveyed could be true or false. Thus it arises when the state of affairs described can be fictitious—when the description may be an exaggeration, or a lie.

It seems that bees are unable to lie, or to exaggerate, although they can, of course, be grossly misled (for example, by experimental scientists). Everything speaks in favor of the conjecture that the bee is so programmed by its genetic instructions that it is impossible for it to express in its dance anything that is contrary to its experience with nectar (or with a more or less promising new home). Thus the most important difference between bee language and human language, I conjecture, is this: the bee is not free to judge—its linguistic expression is the result of the well-interpreted impact of the environment upon the bee's hereditary structure. *But this is not the case with man. Whatever the genetic determinists may say, our linguistic descriptions have a vastly greater degree of freedom.* (It is the freedom not to speak the truth that creates the moral imperative "Speak the truth!"; an imperative that has, like all imperatives, its rare exceptions. Thus we should resist the temptation to admire the bee for its truthfulness: like a thermometer, the bee cannot help telling the truth.[13]

The invention of the human descriptive language, with its quite fundamental freedom of truly describing reality as it is or else of inventing a story, this, I suggest, is the basis of the *human* mind, of the gap between us and our forbears. Animals, I suggest, have their realm of freedom also. But the realm of human freedom is incomparably greater.

In this way, truth becomes a problem; and we learn to search for truth: the beginning of rationality. Language is used not only to describe, but also to argue for the truth or the falsity of a conjecture.

In Table 1, the main functions of language are summed up. (The lower functions are placed below the higher functions.)

Table 1. The Main Functions of Language

	Functions	Values
	(4) Argumentative function	Validity/ invalidity
Man	(3) Descriptive function	Falsity/ truth
Perhaps bees	(2) Signal function	Efficiency/ inefficiency
Animals and plants	(1) Expressive function	Revealing/ not revealing

Of course, the list of these functions is far from exhaustive. Several comments may be made here.

1. The lower functions are always involved in the higher, but not the other way around.

2. It seems that no animal, not even the bee, can describe a state of affairs independently of a pressing situation in which a command, or advice, and therefore a *signal*, is the real business of the communication: the descriptive information is part of the signal whose function is to release or trigger off an action that is *useful here and now*. As opposed to this, human descriptive language can convey information that is

not immediately useful. It may not be useful at all, or only conditionally useful, or useful in a totally different situation from the one in which it was originally uttered. This property of human speech is sometimes called "displacement": the description of an event may sometimes be given long after the event. However, *a story may be freely invented rather than merely displaced.* (It is sometimes said that the bee language is displaced because of the spatio-temporal distance between the feeding event and the bee's dance. I do not agree with this: the bee's dance is a reaction, not to the feeding event but to a situation consisting of its return to its co-workers from its feeding experience. This is a situation that has a spatiotemporal extension.) I should be inclined to characterize the power of human descriptive language to describe a state of affairs independently of its present occurrence or even of its ever having occurred by the label "abstraction" rather than "displacement."

3. The tragic cases of Laura Bridgeman and Helen Keller seem to me of greatest importance for an understanding of human language. Both became blind and deaf before the age of two, and so, of course, were dumb; but they learned to use abstract (see item 2 above) *descriptive statements*, descriptive human language. I suggest that these cases show that there is a genetic basis, a strong inborn need, for using language descriptively, and an inborn talent for acquiring the skill to use it; and also an inborn talent to understand an (abstract) description, and a desire for this kind of information. And I suggest that no animal has this need or this talent. Moreover, I suggest that this need and this talent have a genetic basis, and that this is far more important than any other property of human languages. The fact that deaf children learn to use sign languages shows that the phonetic characteristics of human languages are superficial.

4. It seems to me quite superficial and indeed mistaken to characterize human language by its alleged "duality of patterning," that is to say, by the duality of sounds (phonetic components, phonems), and of words (morphems), the al-

leged smallest units of meaning. First of all, sounds may be also words, as in the English "a" or "I." Second, the smallest meaningful units are statements, descriptions of a state of affairs; of course, words like "water" may be used as statements: "water" may mean "Give me water!"; or else "Here is water!"; or else "I want water, not milk!" (Words that are not used as statements are abstracted from statements.) Third, as we can learn from Chinese characters, it is not essential to human descriptive language to exhibit this kind of duality.

(It is interesting to see the genetic code as (i) four *letters* and (ii) sixty-four *words* [with twenty-one or twenty-two quasi-descriptive meanings]; but also (iii) quasi-sentences, prescribing or programming or rather commanding an open set of virtually infinitely many *genes;* to which we should add (iv) quasi-chapters, that is, *chromosomes* and (v) quasi-books, the set of chromosomes, the *total program* [the genom] which alone has real meaning; and the meaning is not descriptive, but prescriptive.)

5. Far more important than the alleged duality, or rather trinity (or *n*-inity) of patterning is the openness, also possessed by the genetic code: the openness of the descriptive unit (sentence, statement; in the case of the genetic code, the gene) and of the descriptive story. It seems to me unlikely that a closed, genetically based repertoire of calls—warning cries, cries for help, war cries—could be opened up.[14] I suggest instead the following, conjecture—unfortunately completely speculative—concerning the origin of human language.

6. I suggest that the main phonetic apparatus of human language arises not from the closed system of calls (cries), but rather from playful babbling and chatter of mothers with babies and of groups of children; and that the descriptive function—the presentation of states of affairs—arises from make-believe plays, and especially from childish play-acting, from imitating the behavior of adults, which is standard among many mammals: mock fights, mock war cries, also mock cries for help, mock commands; impersonating certain

adults (which may lead to giving them names, perhaps call-names). Play-acting may go with babble and chatter, and may *need* something like a descriptive or explanatory commentary: so may the need for storytelling develop together with the situation in which the descriptive character of the story is clear from the beginning. The descriptive language may be first invented by children as a secret gang language (they sometimes still invent it); it may be taken over by the mothers (similar to inventions by Japanese monkeys[15]); and only later, with modifications, by the men: some languages still indicate the sex of the speaker. And out of the story-telling—or as part of it—and the description of a state of affairs may develop the explanatory story, the myth, the theory. The need for the descriptive story, with its immense biological significance, may in time become genetically fixed. The tremendous superiority, especially in warfare, that a descriptive language gives, creates a new selection pressure, and, perhaps, the astonishingly quick growth of the human brain.[16]

It is very unfortunate that it is hardly possible that a speculative conjecture like the foregoing could ever become testable. Yet even so, it has the advantage of telling us an explanatory story of how things may have happened—how a language may have arisen which from the start would be open, capable of infinite development, stimulating the imagination, and leading to fairy tales, to myths, and to explanatory theories: to "culture."

XIII

Human language is, I suggest, the product of human inventiveness; of the human mind. And the human mind is, in its turn, the product of its products: a feedback effect. One particularly important feedback effect would be the invention of arguments: of *giving reasons* for accepting a story as true, or for rejecting it as false. Another very important feedback effect is the invention of counting. First comes the dual and the plural: one, two, many. Then come the numbers up to five; then come the numbers up to ten. And then comes the invention of the principle that we can make any series of numbers longer by adding one.

Each such step is a linguistic innovation, an invention. And each such step changes our mind—our mental picture of the world, our consciousness.

Thus there is feedback, or interaction, between our language and our mind. And with the growth of our language and of our mind, we can see more and more of our world. Language works like a searchlight: it brings into focus the facts which it describes. Thus language not only interacts with our mind, it helps us to see things which we would never have seen without it. I suggest that early inventions such as the igniting and controlling of fire were made with the help of language. There is at least one good argument in favor of the conjecture that descriptive language is much older than the control of fire: if deprived of language, children are no longer human. Deprivation of language has even a physical effect on them, possibly worse than the deprivation of some vitamin, to say nothing of the devastating mental effect. Children deprived of language are scarcely human, and certainly mentally abnormal. But in a mild climate, nobody is dehumanized by being deprived of fire. In fact, learning a language is the only skill that is vital to us. Learning a language is also a tremendous intellectual achievement, and it is one that all normal children master; probably because it is deeply needed by them (a fact that speaks against the doctrine that there are children of very low innate intelligence).

XIV

About twenty years ago I introduced a theory that divides the universe into three subuniverses which I called World 1, World 2 and World 3.

World 1 is the world of all physical bodies and forces and fields of forces; also of organisms, of our own bodies and their parts, our brains, and all physical, chemical and biological processes in our bodies.

World 2 I call the world of our mind; of conscious experiences, our thoughts, our feelings of elation or depression, our aims, our plans of action.

World 3 I call the world of the products of the human mind, and especially the world of our languages: of our stories, our myths, our explanatory theories; the world of our mathematical and physical theories, and of our technologies; and of our biological and medical theories. But beyond this, also the world of art and of architecture and of music—all of these products of our minds which, I suggest, could never have arisen without human language.

World 3 may be called the world of culture. But my theory stresses the central role played by language in human culture. World 3 comprises all books, all libraries, all theories, including, of course, false theories, and even inconsistent theories.[17]

As indicated before, the human mind lives and grows in interaction with its products—the objects or inmates of World 3. And World 3, in its turn, consists largely of physical objects, such as buildings, and sculptures. These products of the human mind are of course not only inmates of World 3, but also inmates of World 1. But in World 3 there are also symphonies and theories. And symphonies or theories are strangely abstract objects: Beethoven's Ninth is not identical with his manuscript (which may get burned without the Ninth getting burned) or with any or all of the printed copies of the records, or with any or all of its performances. Nor is it identical with human experiences or memories. The situation is analogous to Newton's theory of gravitation.

The objects that constitute World 3 are diverse. There are marble sculptures like those of Michelangelo. These are not only material, physical bodies, but unique physical bodies. The status of paintings, of architectural works of art, and of manuscripts of music is somewhat similar; and so is even the status of rare copies of printed books.

But as a rule, the status of a book as a World 3 object is

utterly different. If I ask a physics student whether he has read Newton's *Optics*, then I do not refer to a material book, and certainly not to a unique physical body, but to the *content* of Newton's thought. And I do not refer to Newton's actual thought processes which of course belong to World 2, but to something far more abstract, to something that belongs to World 3. It is difficult to make this quite clear, but it is very important. The main problem is again the status of a statement, and the logical relations between statements.

I will use as my first example two very simple arithmetical statements:

(1) $47 \times 34 = 1608$
(2) $47 \times 34 = 1588$

You will of course see at once that these two statements contradict each other. That is to say, they are so related that they cannot possibly be both true. One of them at least must be false. In fact, both are false, since, as you can easily check, it so happens that

(3) $47 \times 34 = 1598$

From this it follows that

(4)   "$47 \times 34 = 1598$" is true.

From this it follows further that

(5) $47 \times 34 < 1600$,

and it also follows that

(6)   "$47 \times 34 < 1600$" is true,

and that

(7) "$47 \times 34 = 1600$" is false.

So you have here seven very simple arithemetical statements (four equations and two inequalities; or more precisely, three equations, (1), (2), and (3); two statements about two different equations, (4) and (7); and inequality, (5); and a statement about an inequality, (6). I repeat that with the exception of (1) and (2), all these statements or assertions are true. (For example, (7) is true because "47 × 34 = 1600" is indeed false.)

All this is of course quite obvious. But it illustrates a number of important points.

Statements can stand in logical relations; for example: (a) they can contradict each other, as do (1) and (2); (1) and (3); (2) and (3); (b) from (3) follows logically (4), (5), (6) and (7); and (c) since (3) is true, (4), (5), (6) and (7), which are logical consequences of (3), must be true too.

Now all the logical relations, especially contradictoriness, and logical consequence, are World 3 relations. They are relations holding only between World 3 objects. They are, decidedly, *not* psychological World 2 relations: they hold independently of whether anybody has ever thought about them. On the other hand, they can very easily be "grasped": they can be easily understood; we can, mentally, think it all out in our Worlds 2, and we can experience that it is all obviously and trivially convincing; and this is a World 2 experience. Of course, with more difficult theories, such as physical theories, we can grasp them, understand them, without being convinced, at the same time, that they are true.

Our minds, belonging to World 2, are thus capable of standing in close contact with World 3 objects; but World 2 objects—our subjective experiences—must be clearly distinguished from the objective World 3 statements, theories, conjectures, and open problems.

I have spoken before about the interaction between World 2 and World 3 and I will illustrate this by another arithmetical example.

The sequence of natural numbers, 1, 2, 3, . . . is a human invention, a linguistic invention. But we do not invent the distinction between odd numbers and even numbers: we discover this within the World 3 object—the sequence of natural numbers—which we have produced, or invented.

Similarly, we discover that there are divisible numbers and

prime numbers. And we discover that the prime numbers are at first very frequent—in fact the majority: 2, 3, 5, 7, 11, 13, . . .—but that they soon become rarer and rarer. These are facts which we have not made, but which are unintended and unforeseeable and inescapable consequences of the invention of the sequence of natural numbers. They are objective facts of World 3. That they are unforeseeable may become clear when I point out that there are open problems here. For example, we have found that primes sometimes come in pairs, such as 11 and 13, or 17 and 19, or 29 and 31. These are called twin primes, and they become very rare when we proceed to large numbers. But, in spite of much research, we do not know yet whether twin primes fizzle out completely or whether they come again and again; or in other words, we do not know yet whether or not there exists a greatest pair of twin primes. (The conjecture is that no such greatest pair exists.)

Thus there are open problems in World 3; and we work on discovering these problems, and on attempts to solve them. This shows very clearly the objectivity of World 3, and the way World 2 and World 3 interact.

We can thus distinguish between the often conjectural World 3 knowledge (knowledge in the objective sense) and the World 2 knowledge which we carry in our heads.

XV

The incredible thing about the human mind, about life, evolution, and mental growth is the interaction, the feedback, the give and take, between World 2 and World 3; between our mental growth and the growth of the World 3 which is the result of our endeavors, and which helps us to transcend ourselves, our talents, our gifts.

It is this self-transcendence which is the most important fact of all life and of all evolution. This is the way in which we learn; and we can say that our mind is the light that illuminates nature.

NOTES

1. Karl Popper, *Logic of Scientific Discovery* (New York: Basic Books, 1959), especially Appendix VII; and Karl Popper, *Objective Knowledge: An Evolutionary Approach* (Oxford: Clarendon Press, 1972), pp. 101–103.

2. Karl Popper, *Conjectures and Refutations: The Growth of Scientific Knowledge* (New York: Basic Books, 1962), pp. 223–224.

3. The assumption that the statement is unambiguous is made in order to exclude statements such as: "It is now twelve o'clock" or "I am now speaking English."

4. Hermann Diels-Kranz, *Die Fragmente der Vorsokratiker, griechisch und deutsch*, 21 B 34 (volume I, p. 137). (Xenophanes' four lines are here expanded to six, and "to utter the perfect truth" might be put more literally "to say what is most perfect.") See also Popper, *Conjectures and Refutations*, p. 153.

5. This is perhaps a slight oversimplification, but recombinations can be subsumed under this characterization.

6. Ernst Mayr, *Cold Spring Harbor Symposia on Quantitative Biology* 24 (1959), p. 1. Ernst Mayr also adopted views closely akin to what I call "active Darwinism," however.

7. Karl Popper, *Logik der Forschung: Zur Erkenntnistheorie der modernen Naturwissenschaft* (Wien: Springer, 1935); Karl Popper, *Quantum Theory and the Schism in Physics: From the Postscript to the Logic of Scientific Discovery as edited by W. W. Bartley, III* (Totowa, N.J.: Rowan and Littlefield, 1982).

8. Alister Hardy, *The Living Stream: A Restatement of Evolution Theory and Its Relation to the Spirit of Man* (London: Collins, 1965), especially pp. 161–171.

9. Ibid., pp. 170 ff.

10. Charles Darwin, *On the Origin of the Species by Means of Natural Selection*, 5th ed. (New York: Appleton, 1870); Charles Darwin, *The Origin of the Species*, a variorum text, ed. Morse Peckham (Philadelphia: University of Pennsylvania Press, 1959); Karl R. Popper and John C. Eccles, *The Self and Its Brain* (New York: Springer International, 1977), p. 13.

11. W. H. Thorpe has produced experimental methods of measuring the attraction (or repulsion) that certain smells exert on insects. *Proceedings of the Royal Society of London (Series B: Biological Sciences)*. 124 (1937), p. 56; 126 (1938), p. 370; 127 (1939), p. 424.

12. The bees may take up to five or six days to prepare themselves for swarming, and during this situation, this state of excitement (it is, clearly, *one* situation although it lasts so long), they may be under the influence of the dancing scouts, and ultimately act upon their linguistic description and "advice." This is, I think, unique among animals. But what Buhler intended by his descriptive function was not an *ad hoc* description, relevant just to one confined situation.

13. The worker bee speaks only to its helpmates. This may explain why her genes were selected for truthtelling, while those of some butterflies were selected for mimicry: lying to their predators is widely practiced and, we may conjecture, genetically based. Man, we may speculate, was selected for speaking the truth to helpmates or friends, *and* for storytelling (or lying) to his competitors or enemies. However, I prefer a very different conjecture. See point 6 and footnote 16.

14. That it can is suggested by C. F. Hockett and Robert Ascher, "The Human Revolution," *Current Anthropology* 5 (1964), p. 135; a very excellent article.

15. See John E. Frisch, "Research on Primate Behavior in Japan," American Anthropologist 61 (1959), pp. 584–596.

16. Neotony may perhaps be involved. See also the remarks under point 10 by Weston La Barre in *Current Anthropology* 5 (1964), pp. 149 f.

17. As I have shown at length in *Mind,* 49 (1940), reprinted in *Conjectures and Refutations,* Chapter 15, *anything* follows from a self-contradictory statement, or sentence, or theory. (This fact, although certainly well known to the Warsaw school of logicians, does not seem to have been well known to English speaking logicians before this publication of mine; compare, for example, *The Philosophy of Bertrand Russell,* ed. P. A. Schilpp [La Salle, Illinois: Open Court], 19XX, pp. 695 f. and 264.) This property of contradictions is an interesting fact of logic, and therefore of World 3. A critic in *Mind* (1978) of *The Self and Its Brain* criticized my theory of the World 3 by referring to this logical fact (he does not seem to have known that I was instrumental in making this fact known). But he was simply mistaken in his belief that a difficulty could arise from this logical fact for my theory of World 3: the universe of discourse of statements or of theoretical systems also contains as a matter of course self-contradictory statements or theoretical systems, which creates no difficulty for the calculus of statements or systems.

Mind as Ineffable

RICHARD RORTY

1. "Mind" as a Blur

The question as to the place of Mind in Nature is a reformulation of the question as to the place of human beings in nature. T. H. Huxley's essay on "Man's Place in Nature"[1] was an attempt to break down the distinction between human beings and animals by viewing our species in the light of biological evolution. For most people at least, Huxley settled the question of whether the existence of our species required a different sort of explanation than did the existence of other kinds of animals. But this result simply transferred the problem to philosophy. The question now became: granted that what is special about human beings was produced by the same sorts of causes as produced the special faculties of the other animal species, are these human faculties nonetheless *so* different that there is a special, philosophical, problem about their nature? Granted, in other words, that what we call "mind" came into the world by spatio-temporal mechanisms homogenous with those which produced the rest of the world's contents, what *is* it that we call "mind"? Something which is simply a special case of the other—physical—things which emerged? Or something "irreducible" to the physical?

This is a vague question because "irreducible" is a multiply ambiguous word. Most discussions of "the mind-body problem" argue for reducibility or irreducibility by tacitly choosing a sense, or senses, of "reducible" favorable to their own side. There are many such senses, stretching along a spectrum between a purely causal sense at one end and a purely definitional sense at the other. Those inclined to reduce mind to matter like to think that Huxley's point that mind emerged from matter is enough to show that there can be no ontological discontinuity. So this side employs a sense of "reducible" in which Xs are reducible to Ys if all the causes of Xs are Ys. Those inclined to proclaim the irreducibility of mind like to think that since you cannot communicate what tarragon tastes like by telling a story about molecules there obviously *is* an ontological discontinuity. So they employ a sense of "reducible" in which Xs are reducible to Ys only if somebody who knows everything about Ys also automatically knows everything about Xs.

More judicious philosophers write long books making endless distinctions between various senses of "mental," of "physical," and of "reducible." Such distinctions are necessary to keep discussion of the subject honest, but by the time they are made the philosophers have usually lost their audience. One classic book of this sort—*The Mind and Its Place in Nature*, by C. D. Broad, written in 1923[2]—offers 666 pages of close argumentation. It arrives at conclusions so precise, complex, and tedious as to make one wonder why anybody ever worried about the mind in the first place. Broad congratulates himself on having stripped his subject of human interest. On page 655, he claims to have shown

that there is no special connexion between Mentalism as such and a cheerful view of the prospects of Mind, and no special connexion between Materialism as such and a depressing view of the prospects of Mind.

This conclusion amounts to transforming the "mind-body problem" into a *scholastic* issue—an issue whose outcome doesn't make a difference to anything else, one which only specialists could care about.

Such scholasticism is a recurring danger in philosophy of

mind. The notion of "mind" seems full of excitement and significance at the outset, but by the time philosophers have finished discussing its reducibility or irreducibility, their conclusions seem to have no relation to the initial motivations of inquiry. I think there is a reason for this. It is that the distinction between the mental and the physical, or between mind and body, is a very bad distinction. The question "What is the place of man in nature?" is a good one if it is construed to mean something like: "What self-image should we humans have of ourselves?" For then it is shorthand for Kant's classic questions "What do we know? What should we do? What may we hope?" Darwin and Huxley gave us reason to think that Kant, and the philosophical tradition generally, might have given bad answers to these questions. But the idea that we could refocus these questions, make them susceptible to more precise answers, by zeroing in on the notion of "the mind" turned out to be a mistake. The more one zeroes in, the less there is to discuss.

The reason there is nothing there is that the distinction between mind and body is entirely parasitical upon two other distinctions: the distinction between knowers and non-knowers, and the distinction between the morally relevant and the morally irrelevant. It is important for our self-image to think of ourselves as knowers—distinguished from the brute creation in being intelligent, in acting from knowledge rather than from habit or instinct, in being able to contemplate things far away in space and time. It is also important for our self-image to see our species, and perhaps those species close enough to us to share some special faculty (e.g., being conscious, or feeling pain) as part of a *moral* universe—as things which have either obligations or rights or both. The notion of "mind" looks like a way of bringing these two notions—that of a knower and that of a moral agent or subject—together, of subsuming them under a single, clearer, concept. But it is not. The supposedly clearer concept is just a blur—the sort of thing you get when you lay tracings of two delicate and complicated designs down on top of each other.

To say that the notion of "mind" is a blur which we would be better off without is to say that we have no "intuitions" about mind as such. We do not have any data about the nature of the mental. In particular, we do not have any knowledge of what it is to have a mind by looking inside and inspecting our own. This denial that the mind (or "consciousness" or "subjectivity") is a natural kind—further investigation of which might shed light on knowledge or on morality or both—is characteristic of a tradition which has been dominant in Anglo-Saxon philosophy during the last three decades. I shall call this the Ryle-Dennett tradition. It got underway with Gilbert Ryle's *The Concept of Mind*,[3] and reached its culmination in Daniel Dennett's *Brainstorms*.[4] Dennett's book synthesizes thirty years of work along the lines which Ryle opened up. This work tried to answer the question "how can we say everything we want to say about ourselves—about our cognitive abilities and our moral status—*without* talking about the difference between mind and body?" It substituted this good new question for the bad old question "Is mind, as something determinate and familiar, about which we have considerable data, reducible to matter?" Philosophy of mind, paradoxically enough, became an interesting area of philosophy only when philosophers began to stop taking the notion of "mind" for granted and began asking whether it was a misleading locution.

In earlier periods, the question about the reducibility or irreducibility of mind was linked either with the question "What is the mind such that it can reach beyond itself and know the physical?" or "What is mind such that its possession makes one a member of the moral universe?" or with both. The latter question was characteristic of philosophers who treated "mind" as meaning what the German Idealists had meant by *Geist*. The former was characteristic of philosophers who, under the influence of British Empiricism, were troubled by questions about perception and the relation between "objects immediately present to the mind" and other objects. Both questions presupposed that if one knew more about mind, if one zeroed in upon its nature, then one would know more about either what Locke had called "the original, certainty and extent of human knowledge" or what Hegel had called "the Idea become conscious of itself," or both. By denying that we had independent information about our mental states which would cast light on either of these matters, the Ryle-Dennett tradition made it possible to talk about such things as beliefs and pains without talking about the mind. That is, it made it possible to develop accounts of what beliefs and pains were which disregarded the question "Are they mental entities or physical entities?"

This tradition thus was able to focus on the question of what psychologists were up to without getting involved with bad questions about the legitimacy of "behavioristic" or "introspective" methods. It was also able to take the advent of computers in its stride, by refusing to be buffaloed by the question "Do these machines really *think?*" "Can they *really* feel?" These virtues were attained by its refusal to think that anything vastly important turned on the answer to these questions—that matters of epistemological or moral moment were involved in psychologists' research programs, or in the success of veiled computers in fooling people into thinking that they were human. In my view, this tradition is one of the few successes of which analytic philosophy can boast—one of the few recent cases in which philosophy professors have actually performed a service for culture as a whole. They performed it by getting us out from under a lot of bad questions, of bad, scholastic answers to such questions, and of misleading rhetoric based on such bad answers.

This tradition has, however, recently come under attack. Furthermore, it has come under attack at just the point at which it most firmly separated itself from pre-Rylean work in the area—its claim that we have no intuitions about the mind as such. In a reaction against the Ryle-Dennett tradition as "verificationist" and "reductionist," philosophers like Thomas Nagel and John Searle have been trying to turn the clock back to the days of Broad. Broad thought it enough to refute behaviorism to say such things as:

It is plain that our observation of the behavior of external bodies is not our only or our primary ground for asserting the existence of minds or mental processes. . . .[5]

If we confine ourselves to bodily behavior it is perfectly certain that we are leaving out something of whose existence *we are immediately aware* in favorable cases.[6] (Italics added.)

Similarly, Nagel thinks it enough to appeal to our immediate awareness of "what it is like to be us" in order to establish an ontological divide between "the subjective" and "the objective":

A feature of experience is subjective if it can in principle be fully understood only from one *type* of point of view: that of a being like the one having the experience, or at least like it in the relevant modality. The phenomenological qualities of our experience are subjective in this way. The physical events in our brain are not.[7]

Nagel thinks, like Broad, that there are different "referential paths" leading to our use of the term "pain" on the one hand and to our use of terms like "stimulated C-fibers" on the other. He thinks the suggestion that the two terms refer to the same thing unintelligible:

At the present time the status of physicalism is similar to that which the hypothesis that matter is energy would have had if uttered by a pre-Socratic philosopher. We do not have the beginnings of a conception of how it might be true. . . . The idea of how a mental and a physical term might refer to the same thing is lacking, and the usual analogies with theoretical identification in other fields fail to supply it.[8]

They fail, Nagel thinks, because the only true account of "the referential path" for terms like "pain" is one which goes through the sort of "direct awareness" of which Broad speaks.

2. Redescribing the Known and Redescribing the Knower

My main concern in this paper will be to defend the Ryle-Dennett tradition against Nagel's revival of the notion of our direct acquaintance with our minds, the idea that we have ontological intuitions which make the notion of "mind" more than just a blur. But before confronting this question directly, I think it will be helpful to put the issue in a broader perspective by considering the history of what A.O. Lovejoy called "revolts against dualism." Lovejoy, writing in 1930, said that the past quarter-century of philosophy had been "the Age of the Great Revolt Against Dualism . . . a phase of a wider Revolt of the Twentieth Century Against the Seventeenth."[9] This revolt was, he said,

an attempt to escape from the double dualism which the seventeenth-century philosophers did not, indeed, originate, but to which they gave reasoned and methodical expression—the epistemological dualism of the theory of representative perception and the psychophysical dualism which conceives empirical reality to fall asunder into a world of mind and a world of matter mutually exclusive and utterly antithetic.[10]

Lovejoy thought that the first dualism was the root of the second, and that people were, rightly, led to accept epistemological dualism

simply because they have formed certain preconceptions as to what an object of knowledge ought to be, and then, comparing the characteristics of the thing directly presented in their experience with these preconceptions, have found that the two do not match.[11]

Most of the revolts which Lovejoy discussed were attempts to say that these preconceptions about what an object of knowledge ought to be were false. Whereas common sense, according to Lovejoy, suggests that most of the things we want to know about are quite unlike the sort of thing which we find "before the mind," anti-dualistic philosophers like James, Dewey, Whitehead, and Russell insisted that they were much the same.

These philosophers argued in two ways: some, like Russell, said that we were directly aware of physical objects, that the "data of experience" themselves had a place in the physical world. Others, like Whitehead, said that the normal conception of a physical object as something ontologically distinct from experiences was a "fallacy of misplaced concreteness," and argued for panpsychism. Both of these lines of argument agreed, however, in taking the notion of a "datum of experience"—of something "directly presented in experience"—at face value. Russell and Whitehead both wanted to unify the "stuff" of the world, rather than letting it be divided into nonspatial mind and spatial matter. The point of doing so was to redescribe the sort of stuff which is "out there" so that it turns out to be the same stuff which is "before our minds." Finding such a stuff was the object of the exercise. In a phrase of Austin's, these anti-Cartesian philosophers took as their starting-point "the ontology of the sensible manifold"—the Kantian view that something primordial and homogenous was *intuited*, prior to the employment of *concepts* to mark off this manifold into mental and physical sectors. If one could describe the world in terms of relations between bits of this more basic stuff—e.g., Russell's "views" or Whitehead's "prehensions"—then there would no longer be a contrast between cognoscenda and data, between "what an object of knowledge ought to be" and "the characteristics of the thing directly presented in experience." Thus there would be no problem of knowledge. Nothing would remain of what Lovejoy described as

the seeming mystery and challenging paradox of knowledge—the possibility which it implies of going abroad while keeping at home, the knower's apparent transcendence of the existential limits within which he must yet, at every moment of his knowing, confess himself to be contained.[12]

This pre-Rylean revolt against dualism, then, was entirely motivated by epistemological considerations, and never questioned the initial assumption that there was *something* "directly presented to the mind." The epistemological problematic which Russell and Whitehead confronted was, like Kant's, a matter of bridging the gap which Descartes had seemed to open up—the gap between the immediately known and the inferentially known. Their solutions thus belong to a genre which includes Leibniz's monadism, Spinoza's double-aspect theory, Berkeley's phenomenalism, Kant's own transcendental idealism, Hegel's notion of the progressive development of self-consciousness as the progressive overcoming of the subject-object distinction, James's "world of pure experience," Ayer's notion of minds and physical objects as "logical constructions," and so on. This genre might be dubbed "Cartesian metaphysics," referring not to Descartes's own dualistic metaphysics but to the genre which arose out of accepting Descartes's notion of "immediate presence" to the mind, while trying to avoid the skeptical consequences which ensued (by some less *ad hoc* procedure than Descartes's appeal to divine benevolence.)

By contrast, Ryle's revolt against Descartes was not an attempt to redescribe the inferentially known in order to make it homogeneous with the immediately known. Rather, it was an attempt to undercut the original Cartesian notion of the mind as the immediately knowable, the given. It belongs to the anti-Cartesian tradition which includes Reid's complaints against "the way of ideas," neo-Thomist protests against the doctrine of representative perception, and phenomenologists' insistence on the intentionality of consciousness. It attacks the assumption which Cartesian metaphysics never questioned, the assumption that there is something "directly present to consciousness," immediately before the eye of the mind, and that we know what sort of thing that is because it is itself *mental* in nature.

The way in which Ryle questioned this assumption was to question whether we had any privileged access to our inner states. Ryle denied this, saying:

The sorts of things that I can find out about myself are the same as the sorts of things that I can find out about other people, and the methods of finding them out are much the same. A residual difference in the supplies of the requisite data makes some difference in degree between what I can know about myself and what I can know about you, but these differences are not all in favor of self-knowledge.[13]

Ryle said that once we appreciate this point we could get rid of the notion that "The things that a mind does or experiences are self-intimating" and that mental events are such that "it is part of the definition of their being mental that their occurrence entails that they are self-intimating."[14] Ryle summed up as follows:

The radical objection to the theory that minds must know what they are about, because mental happenings are by definition conscious, or metaphorically self-luminous, is that there are no such happenings. . . .[15]

But he then seemed to contradict himself by admitting that there were such things as introspectible events—as when he said that the only reason why I might know more about my intellect and character than you do is that "I am the addressee of my unspoken soliloquies."[16] His critics jumped on such passages to show that the notion of a train of introspectible inner events—conscious experiences—was being presupposed even by an author who claimed not to believe there were such things.

These critics were justified, and in retrospect we can see that Ryle got off on the wrong foot in questioning the existence of introspection. What he should have said, and what others (such as Sellars) did say, was that our knowledge of what we are like on the inside is no more "direct" or "intuitive" than our knowledge of what things are like in the "external world." For knowledge to be "direct" is simply for it be gained without going through an introspectible process of inference—so that we know with *equal* directness that we feel nostalgic, that something before us is brown, that it is a table, that it is the table that used to stand next to the fireplace in our childhood home, and so on. We no more know "the nature of mind" by introspecting mental events than we know "the nature of matter" by perceiving tables. To know the nature of something is not a matter of having it before the mind, of intuiting it, but of being able to utter a large number of true propositions about it.

If one takes this view of knowledge, and in particular of

"intuitive" knowledge, then one will be able to say that, *pace* Ryle, there really is a set of mental events going on inside us, and that in defining them as "mental" we are, indeed, saying that we cannot help but be aware of them when they occur. But this admission will not lead us to think that Descartes was right; that we have an extra added ingredient called a "mind" in addition to our bodies. To suggest that we do is to suggest something which we could not possibly know by intuition— namely, that when science finally breaks our bodies down into their finest-grained spatial components it will not be able to explain how we work without postulating the existence of something different than those components. This is a conjecture which we are not now in a position to test—simply because our instruments are too gross to grapple effectively with our brain. But whether this conjecture is true has nothing to do with the traditional bad, ambiguous, philosophical, armchair, question of whether mental events are "reducible" to physical events.

Once this Wittgensteinian-Sellarsian epistemological point was made, the essential step in revolting against Cartesian dualism was accomplished. For the central notion of epistemological dualism (upon which, as Lovejoy rightly claimed, psychophysical dualism rests) is now discarded. Taking this step amounts to saying: we already know all about the nature of knowledge without knowing anything new, or deep, about the mind. To think of knowledge as a matter of being disposed to utter true sentences about something, rather than in terms of the metaphor of "acquaintance" —to think of our knowledge of objects as identical with our knowledge of the truth of propositions about them rather than as a pre-linguistic precondition for such knowledge—is to enable us to stop thinking of ourselves as divided into two parts, a mental part and physical part. For now we are able to describe the gap between ourselves and the beasts, in respect of intelligence, not as a matter of our having additional faculties, but simply as a matter of our behaving in more complex ways—more specifically, as exhibiting *linguistic* behavior. On this "psychological nominalist" view (in Sellars's phrase), Lovejoy is just wrong in saying that knowledge involves "a seeming mystery and challenging paradox." Lovejoy thought it wondrous that starting with visual images we could get to tables, since the introspectible "data" were so very different from the spatial cognoscenda. But the reply is that we do not start with visual images. We do not "start" with *anything*. We just are trained to make reports—some perceptual, some introspective—as part of our general training in uttering true sentences; our learning of the language. There is no more or less mystery and paradox in our species having learned to manipulate sentences than in bower-birds having learned to manipulate plant stems and vines. Huxley and Darwin thus turn out to have told us all we need to know about our place in nature—for what needs to be explained is simply our *behavior*. Once we know all about our behavior we shall automatically know all about our nature and our place. This was the anti-Cartesian result which Ryle wanted to get, and he was right in wanting this, even though the strategy he used was wrong.

To sum up what I have been saying in this section: the second, Rylean, behaviorist revolt against dualism, construed in a Wittgensteinian and Sellarsian way, succeeded where the first revolt—that of Cartesian metaphysics—had failed. For the second revolt undercut the premise which the first kind of revolt shared with Descartes himself: the premise that we have intuitive knowledge, knowledge which is pre-linguistic and which thus serves as a test for the adequacy of languages.

3. Behaviorism, Materialism, and Functionalism

The history of philosophy of mind since Ryle has been one of fratricidal quarrels among philosophers who agreed, for the most part, in accepting the anti-Cartesian analysis of knowledge which I have just sketched, but who nonetheless managed to quarrel. They quarreled because they took it to be the task of the philosophy of mind to answer the question "What are mental states?" This, like the question "What is the nature of the mind?" is not a good question. The trouble is that there are too many different sorts of mental states. These philosophers wanted a nice short answer to their question which would cover everything that anybody had ever called "mental," or at least anything which a psychologist might want to investigate. In particular, they wanted to cover both pains and beliefs. Trying to find a neat way of characterizing what a toothache and a theological conviction have in common is as unpromising as attempting to find a characterization of "physical event" which covers both the death of a partridge and the polarization of a beam of electrons. If, following up the suggestion made above, one takes the definition of mental to be "introspectible" then one will have no trouble with toothaches but lots of trouble with beliefs. For we seem to have lots of beliefs we don't *know* we have. If one follows Kant's lead and suggests that since partridges and electrons both have spatial locations, maybe mental states are nonspatial, one has trouble with toothaches, which seems about as spatial as you can get. But philosophers of mind, undaunted by these difficulties, proceeded to announce either that mental states were "dispositions to behave" (Ryle et al.) or "states of the brain" (Smart et al.) or "functional states" (Putnam et al.).[17]

These announcements gave rise to three "isms"—"logical behaviorism," "central-state materialism," and "functionalism." The proponents of these views had very little to disagree about, but managed it nevertheless. The logical behaviorists said that to say that a person believed that *p* was to say that, *ceteris paribus*, he would act in certain ways, including saying certain things. To say that he had a toothache was to say the same sort of thing. This claim was attacked on two grounds. First, nobody can give necessary and sufficient behavioral conditions for the truth of "Flynn has a toothache" or "Flynn has Docetist views about the operation of Grace." Second, it seems as odd to say that a toothache is a *disposition* to behave as that a battered nerve is a *disposition* to behave. It would seem more natural to say that both are *causes* of behavior.

This second line of attack led to the popularity of "central-state materialism." Philosophers of this persuasion said that whatever else a toothache was it was the cause of behavior, that a stimulated nerve was the cause of the same behavior, and that Occam's razor suggested that we view "toothache" and "stimulation of such-n-such a nerve" as two names for the same thing. When it was objected that toothaches don't *feel* like battered nerves, the central-state materialists asked, reasonably enough, how one could possibly know that it didn't. Why shouldn't the way a toothache feels *be* the way the stimulation of a certain nerve feels? How would one *expect* such a stimulation to feel?

There was, however, another objection to central-state materialism which was not so easy to dispose of. This was that it sounded much more plausible for toothaches than for beliefs. To say that Flynn's belief in the Docetist heresy is a state of his brain ought to imply that everybody who believes that particular heresy has a brain that is in that same state. But, as Putnam and others remarked, there seems nothing to prevent a Martian or a robot having this heretical view even though their brains are made out of different stuff, or wired up differently than ours. So Putnam suggested, pursuing the analogy with computers, that mental states were functional states—"program" or "software" states—as opposed to the "hardware" brain states. This looked to many people like simply veering back to Rylean "behavioral dispositions." But although functionalism certainly was a move in this direction, it was an advance on Ryle. It avoided the first objection to logical behaviorism which I listed above. It did not require that necessary and sufficient behavioral conditions be given for the ascription of beliefs or pains. Rather, the functionalists said, to say that a given state of an organism is a belief of a certain sort is no more to say something about what the organism will do under certain conditions, than to say a computer is running a certain program is to say that it will generate output X if it gets input Y. For many *different* programs will have that feature. So, the functionalists said, we now have a nonreductive account of the mental, since we recognize that the meaning of mentalistic terms cannot be "reduced," but must be explained in *other* mentalistic terms.

This jerky movement from logical behaviorism to central-state materialism to functionalism was pushed along by successive realizations that what you say about pain doesn't work for belief, and vice versa. The final synthesis of this antinomy is, I think, offered by Putnam. In answer to the charge that functionalism doesn't catch the raw awfulness of pain, the felt excruciatingness, what it is *like* to be in pain, Putnam simply identifies the particular way a given pain feels with the particular physical realization of the functional state "being in pain" which the subject has. Putnam imagines a case in which somebody's spectrum is inverted. Here one is inclined to say that the mental state which now triggers his response "that's blue" (once the person has gotten used to the fact that blue things now look the way yellow things used to) is functionally identical but *qualitatively* different from the mental state which triggered the response before the inversion. Putnam says:

It seems to me that the most plausible move for a functionalist to make, if such cases are really possible, is to say "Yes, but the 'qualitative character' just is the physical realization." And to say that for this special kind of psychological property, for *qualities*, the older form of the identity theory was the right one.[18]

In other words, Putnam is saying: what resists being treated as software should be treated as hardware, and conversely. The upshot of functionalism is thus a casual syncretism. Functionalism comes down to saying that anything you want to say about persons will have an analogue in something you can say about computers, and that if you know as much about a person as a team consisting of the ideal design engineer and the ideal programmer know about a computer, then you know *all* there is to know about the person. So what a team made up of the ideal physiologist and the ideal Miller-Galanter-Pribram "cognitive psychologist" would know is *all* there is to know about people, and, *a fortiori*, about their minds.

This pragmatical attitude towards persons and minds is, I think, the upshot of the last thirty years of work in the philosophy of mind. Its clearest expression is Dennett's "homuncular functionalism," which says that the basic strategy of psychological explanation is for the psychologist to postulate little believers, desirers, feelers of pain, decision-makers, and the like inside the person, and then to postulate similar homunculi inside of *them*, and so on down through layers of simpler and stupider homunculi until you hit a homunculus so simple and stupid that your colleague in physiology can identify it with something he knows about— e.g., a certain type of neuron. No mysteries remain about how a computer does something when we break its program down into a flow chart so finely grained that the littlest boxes are recognizable as a particular, simple, electrical circuit. Similarly, in Dennett's view, no mysteries would remain about people if we had a flow chart for them—one whose smallest boxes were recognizable as a particular, simple neural circuit.

On my account, then, homuncular functionalism is a happy blend of all that was best in logical behaviorism and all that was best in central-state materialism. However, to adopt it is not, as Putnam once thought, to have a new and enlightening answer to the question "What are mental states?" For to say that they are *functional* states is trivial. Every state of anything is a functional state. To say that an entity E may have a functional state S is just to say that E can be described in one vocabulary, V_1, which is relatively fine-grained, and another, V_2, which is relatively coarse-grained, that some descriptions of E in V_2 can be correlated with sets of descriptions of E in V_1 the former, and that "S" is in V_2. For any E and any S, with one can find a vocabulary which plays the role of V_1 with the possible exception of some states of elementary particles, one can find a vocabulary which plays the role of V_1 with respect to the vocabulary in which "S" occurs. The force of Putnam's and Dennett's functionalism is not to have discovered the nature of mental states, but to say that they don't have a nature—or, if you like, to say that mental states are those functional states which are investigated by the psychologists, as opposed to those investigated by the physiologists. Mental states are simply those whose descriptions occur in a *given* vocabulary used by psychologists, the one that contains, e.g., both "belief" and "pain." The question whether this is the *right* vocabulary to describe these states is as silly as the question of whether these *states* are really mental, or rather are physical states in disguise.

There is no deep reason why we should lump pains and beliefs together, rather than lumping both in with nerve-stimulations, or lumping pains with the stimulations of nerves and other beliefs with states of supernatural Grace. But our clumsy efforts to predict and control ourselves have given rise to a discipline—psychology—which has taken both pains and beliefs in its charge. At the moment, at least, there seems no reason to portion things out differently. So we can content ourselves with saying that the nature of a mental state is to be the sort of state of the human organism which psychologists study. This sort of definition has the same advantage as does defining legal, as opposed to moral responsibility, as the sort of responsibility which the courts are willing to adjudicate. Such definitions remind us that distinctions like legal-vs.-moral, or mental-vs.-physical, are not written on the face of the world. Rather, they are cultural artifacts, to be judged by their utility in accomplishing our aims.

To take this nominalist view is to carry through on the Rylean-Wittgensteinian-Sellarsian attitude towards knowledge which, in the previous section, I claimed was the rationale of the "second" revolt against dualism. Once again, I want to urge that the upshot of this second revolt is not to have given us a clearer view of "the nature of the mind" or of "our concept of mind," but merely to have enabled us to give up the attempt to find real essences in the area. We have been freed from this need by the realization that Descartes was wrong in saying that "nothing is easier for the mind to know than itself," and Broad wrong in saying that behaviorism "leaves out something of whose existence we are immediately aware." Debunking this Cartesian notion of immediate awareness is not the effect of a better philosophical understanding of mind. Rather it is the cause of our ceasing to ask for a "better philosophical understanding of mind," of our ceasing to ask certain bad questions.

4. Dennett's Nominalism versus Searle's and Nagel's Essentialism

The issue between the Descartes-Broad tradition and the Ryle-Dennett tradition comes into focus in the following passage from Dennett:

Any philosopher of mind who (like myself) favors a "functionalist" theory of mind must face the fact that the very feature that has been seen to recommend functionalism over cruder brands of materialism—its abstractness and hence neutrality with regard to what could "realize" the function deemed essential to sentient or intentional systems—permits a functionalist theory, however realistically biological or humanoid in flavor, to be instantiated not only by robots (an acceptable or even desirable consequence in the eyes of some), but by suprahuman organizations that would seem to have minds of their own only in the flimsiest metaphorical sense.[19]

As Dennett goes on to say, the problem is that functionalism (and, indeed pretty well any imaginable psychological account) is going to give an account of pain or belief in terms of entities which aren't themselves "subjects of experience" —entities at what Dennett calls a "sub-personal level." "Intuition," Dennett continues,

proclaims that any sub-personal theory must leave out something vital, something unobtainable moreover with subpersonal resources.[20]

Any account of pain or belief which gives you a flow chart is going to be met with the objection that nothing on the flow chart is a believer or a feeler of pain, and thus that the total system which the flow chart purports to analyze cannot be either.

John Searle has made this objection in the case of "intentionality":

No purely formal model will ever be sufficient by itself for intentionality because the formal properties are not by themselves constitutive of intentionality, and they have by themselves no causal power except the power, when instantiated, to produce the next stage of the formalism when the machine is running. . . .

All the arguments for the strong version of artificial intelligence that I have seen insist on drawing an outline around the shadows cast by cognition and then claiming that the shadows are the real thing.[21]

If we are to conclude that there must be cognition in me on the grounds that I have a certain sort of input and output and a program in between, then it looks like all sorts of apparently noncognitive subsystems are going to turn out to be cognitive.[22]

The proper nominalist response to this is that the word "cognitive" applies to whatever psychologists say it applies to—that is, to whatever their best account of cognition leads them to call a cognitive process. But Searle will have none of that. He says:

. . . the mental-nonmental distinction cannot be just in the eye of the beholder but it must be intrinsic to the systems, otherwise it would be up to any beholder to treat people as nonmental and, for example, hurricanes as mental if he likes.[23]

Thomas Nagel mounts the same objection as does Searle, focusing on pains rather than on beliefs. Like Searle, Nagel believes that words like "pain," "belief," "cognition," "conscious," and "mental" signify real essences, that they are not just convenient handles to get a grip on what's going on. Nagel's objection to flow chart accounts of pain and belief, of the sort which Dennett gives, is that

Certainly it *appears* unlikely that we will get closer to the real nature of human experience by leaving behind the particularity of our human point of view and striving for a description in terms accessible to beings that could not imagine what it was like to be us.[24]

More generally, Nagel says:

We appear to be faced with a general difficulty about psychophysical reduction. In other areas the process of reduction is a move in the direction of greater objectivity, toward a more accurate view of the real nature of things. . . . Experience, however, does not seem to fit the pattern. The idea of moving from appearance to reality seems to make no sense here. What is the analogue in this case to pursuing a more objective understanding of the same phenomena by abandoning the initial subjective viewpoint toward them in favor of another that is more objective but concerns the same thing?[25]

It is important to see that Nagel's and Searle's disagreement with Dennett is not about the nature of the mind but about the nature of explanation and objectivity. The nominalist approach to the distinctions between appearance and reality, subjective and objective, is to say that these are misleading ways of formulating the distinction between a vocabulary which doesn't help you get what you want and a vocabulary which does. This approach is based on a philosophy of science which is Baconian, Hobbesian and Galilean rather than, like Nagel's and Searle's, Aristotelian. On an Aristotelian view, Galileo's account of motion is absurdly counter-intuitive, as are, for example, contemporary biochemistry's account of life, Feuerbach's and Tillich's accounts of God, and utilitarians' accounts of morality. For the Aristotelian thinks that we need to distinguish between discovering the nature of something and discovering a vocabulary which will permit us to predict and control events in the area of the thing. The nominalist, on the other hand, construes "finding the nature of X" as just finding the most useful way to talk about the things which have traditionally been called "X"—a way which need not employ any term coreferential with "X."[26]

Dennett takes this nominalist line when he rejects the assumption that

> our ordinary way of picking out putative mental features and entities succeed in picking out real features and entities . . . most if not all of our familiar mentalistic idioms fail to perform this task of perspicuous reference, because they embody conceptual infelicities and incoherencies of various sorts.[27]

This is just the sort of thing which Galileo said about the jargon of Aristotelian physics. Dennett's claim, however, seems the more paradoxical. In part this is because we forget how very paradoxical Galileo's appeared to many of his contemporaries. But mainly it is because of our conviction that we *cannot* have failed to refer perspicuously to the mental, because "nothing is easier for the mind to know than itself." This Cartesian myth is enshrined in Nagel's claim that "every subjective phenomenon is essentially connected with a point of view, and it seems inevitable than an objective, physical theory will abandon that point of view." "Essential connection with a point of view" is just another name for that specially intimate relationship which Broad called "immediate awareness." Nagel's visual metaphor is a variation on the standard Cartesian metaphor of "directly present to consciousness," the metaphor which Ryle derided as the notion of "contemplation of events in an inner arena."

Perhaps the best way to express the relevant difference between nominalism and essentialism is to take up Searle's point that functionalist flow charts of the sort which Dennett constructs merely "draw an outline around the shadows cast by cognition." The question at issue is whether there is a contrast between shadow and substance—between grasping the causal relations which X bears to other things and grasping what X is in itself, its real essence. The view that there *is not* is a species of the view often, though somewhat misleadingly, called "verificationism." The view that there *is* a contrast is a species of what is often, somewhat misleadingly, called "realism." "Verificationism," in this generic sense, is the view that you know about the nature of X when you know the inferential relationships which are generally agreed to hold between sentences using the word "X" and the other sentences of the language. On this view, you may always learn more about the nature of X, because new scientific developments (for example) may bring about agreement upon new such relationships. But there is nothing beyond such relationships to be discovered. For realists, there is a real essence to be discovered and, since reference swings free of agreement in belief, the nominalists' inferential relationships (the contemporary counterpart of Locke's "nominal essence") may have nothing to do with real essence.

The Nagel-Searle view that we have prelinguistic knowledge of real essence which is not caught in our knowledge of the truth of propositions, is a special case of realism. Searle's view is that intentionality is "intrinsic" and that we can tell it from its shadows, even though the shadows include everything psychologists think relevant to the use of the word "intentionality." Verificationists think that to say, with Searle, that we shall not know what intentionality "really is" until we know more about the brain is an attempt to make a distinction of kind out of a distinction of degree. On their view, we shall of course know *more* about intentionality when we can realize any given flow chart with neural tissue instead of bits of metal and silicon, but we won't know what intentionality "really is" in a sense in which we hadn't known this previously. Similarly, verificationists think it merely tautologous to say, as Nagel does, that "the subjective character of experience" is not captured by "any of the familiar recently devised reductive analyses of the mental, for all of them are logical compatible with its absence."[28] *Of course* no analysis could capture what Nagel calls "the subjective character of experience" since he has *defined* this character as what "human language" is inadequate to express.[29] Nagel thinks that "we can be compelled to recognize the existence of such facts without being able to state or comprehend them."[30] There could be no clearer expression of what the verificationist denies.

To see that the question about verificationism, about the

reach of human language, is the real issue between Dennett and Nagel, consider Dennett's own description of how he deals with anti-functionalist intuitions such as Nagel's. Dennett thinks that there is "a better course than mere doctrinaire verificationism on the one hand or shoulder-shrugging agnosticism on the other."[31] He describes this better course as follows:

What convinces *me* that a cognitivistic theory could capture all the dear features I discover in my inner life is not any "argument," and not just the programmatic appeal of thereby preserving something like "the unity of science," but rather a detailed attempt to describe to myself exactly those features of my life *and the nature of my acquaintance with them* that I would cite as my grounds for claiming that I *am*—and do not merely *seem to be*—conscious.[32]

Dennett, in other words, thinks that he can beat Nagel at his own phenomenological game. He thinks that looking inward and noticing what goes on will help settle the question. Thus when he discusses mental images, and in particular a psychological experiment in which subjects typically say "I rotated the image in my mind's eye," he says:

Now how can my view possibly accommodate such phenomena? Aren't we directly aware of an image rotating in phenomenal space in this instance? No. And that much, I think, you can quickly ascertain to your own satisfaction. For isn't it the case that if you attend to your experience more closely when you say you rotate the image you find it moves in discrete jumps—it flicks through a series of orientations. You cannot gradually speed up or slow down the rotation, can you? *Now "look" again. Isn't it really just that these discrete states are discrete propositional episodes?*[33] (Italics added.)

This last appeal, to introspect and see whether you are introspecting movement or just making judgments, or both, seems to me the wrong move to make. The issue about whether to think of any kind of "looking and seeing" —introspective or observational—as the acquisition of a belief (the sort of analysis offered by Armstrong and Pitcher), or as something "more" than this, is not one which is itself going to be settled by looking and seeing. It is to be settled by considering whether the latter view does any explanatory work left undone by the former.

To make this point a little more precise, consider Dennett's argument that

If you are inclined to argue that only an internal system that actually did proceed by some rotation in space of a representation or image could explain the sequence of judgments, you might be right, but your grounds are hardly overwhelming. In fact these discrete series of judgments bear a striking resemblance to the discrete series of small flashing lights that create the illusions of perceived motion, which have received so much attention from psychologists. . . . What I am suggesting is that as the discrete series of flashes is to that non-veridical judgment, so our series of judgments in the image rotation case is to the judgment that something is rotated in our minds. . . . There *may* be something "behind" our judgments in the rotation case, but if there is, it is something quite outside our present ken, and its very existence is suggested only by the most tenuous inference, however psychologically irresistible it may be.[34]

Dennett is saying that our introspectively based claim that there is a rotating image is intelligible, but is not the only, or the most likely explanation, of the judgments we make. What he should say, on my view, is that in both the case of veridical *and* nonveridical, perceptual or introspective, judgment, the claim that there is something "more" than the acquisition of belief—something not locatable in public space which explains the acquisition—is not an explanation at all. It is just a wave of the hand. To say that "there *may* be something" behind "our judgments in the rotation case" is right if it means merely "there is doubtless some neural set-up which makes clear why we have that series of judgments." But it is wrong if it means that there is some antecedent probability that that neural set-up will be the rotation of something.

I have staged this little skirmish with Dennett simply in order to show why I think that the best strategy to use against Nagel and Searle is what Dennett calls "a doctrinaire verificationism." Dennett thinks that one can be skeptical about

Nagel's insistence on the phenomenologically rich inner lives of bats "without thereby becoming the Village Verificationist." I do not. I think that skepticism about Nagel- and Searle-like intuitions is plausible only if it is based on general methodological considerations about the status of intuitions. The verificationist's general complaint about the realist is that he is insisting on differences (between, e.g., bats with private lives and bats without, dogs with intrinsic intentionality and dogs without) which make no difference: that his intuitions cannot be integrated into an explanatory scheme because they are "wheels which play no part in the mechanism."[35] This seems to me a good complaint to make, and the only one we need make. It amounts to saying that we are going to have to pick and choose among our intuitions in the interest of scientific progress, and that the test of whether an intuition is worth hanging on to is whether it can be integrated into the best theories we currently have. This holistic view of knowledge may be doctrinaire, but surely it is no more so than, for example, Searle's remark that:

> The study of mind starts with such facts as that humans have beliefs, while thermostats, telephones, and adding machines don't. If you get a theory that denies this point you have produced a counter-example to the theory and the theory is false.[36]

This brings back memories of the view that the study of the heavens starts with such facts as that the sun moves around in circles and that the earth is at rest.

5. Mind as Ineffable

I said earlier that the central claim of the Ryle-Dennett tradition was that we had no intuitions, no "initial facts" which all theorizing must always respect, about the mind. It should now be clear that I mean this not as a remark about the mind but as a remark about intuitions—it is a methodological strategy rather than an introspective report. The claim that "mind" is not a useful concept, that the mental-physical contrast is an awkward and clumsy one which the philosophical tradition has wasted too much time on, is not the sort of claim that can itself be backed up by intuitions. It can only be backed up by general considerations about whether language is the sort of thing which can be judged adequate or inadequate to prior, intuitive, nonlinguistic knowledge (as Nagel thinks), or whether the notion of such a comparison between language and the data is empty. On the interpretation of recent developments in the philosophy of mind which I have been offering, the Ryle-Dennett tradition simply works out the consequences of the nominalist view that language is ubiquitous—that there is no such thing as comparing linguistic formulation with a bit of nonlinguistic knowledge, but only a matter of seeing how various linguistic items fit together with other linguistic items and with the purposes for which language as a whole is to be used.

I have argued in favor of this nominalist view on other occasions,[37] and cannot repeat these arguments in the present space. Rather, I should like to conclude by returning to my initial claim that our concept of mind is a blur. When one has a large and blurry concept on one's hands, one can either discard it in favor of a series of smaller, handier, more useful concepts, or one can say that this very largeness and blurriness is a symptom of something *deep* and hard to articulate, something *ineffable*, something to which language is inadequate. The concept "God," as it is used in the sophisticated discourse of Christian theology, is an example. This concept, I should argue, is a result of laying a number of concepts—those of an omnipotent atemporal creator, a stern father, and a loving friend—on top of each other, producing a blur. It is no wonder that a concept which is of being both "without parts or passions" and "closer than hands or feet" should tempt village atheists to discard it. Nor is it any wonder that others have proclaimed it a deep mystery. I want to suggest (following Feurbach) that the concept of mind is the blur with which Western intellectuals became obsessed when they finally gave up on the blur which was the theologian's concept of God.

The ineffability of the mental serves the same cultural function as the ineffability of the divine—it vaguely suggests that science does not have the last word.[38]

I cannot, in the present space, provide the historical backup which this claim requires. But I would ask you to think of the way in which German Idealism's notion of *Geist* came to be the watchword of a reaction against scientism, a way of recapturing, or making intellectually respectable, what religion had posessed and the Enlightenment seemed to have lost. In Hegel, and again in the British and American idealists of the turn of the century, we find the distinction between Spirit and Nature doing the job which used to be done by the distinction between the Divine and the Human. The Spirit-Nature distinction attempts to synthesize, and succeeds in blurring, the two distinctions upon which, I have claimed, the mental-physical distinction is parasitic: that between the cognitive and the noncognitive and that between the moral and the non-moral. Philosophers in the naturalist, anti-idealist tradition (such as Russell, Whitehead, James, and Dewey) took the notion of "the mind" seriously because they felt they had to show that cognition was possible without our possession of an "extra added ingredient" of the sort which would serve as an "ontological foundation for morality." But unfortunately they thought that ordinary vulgar materialism —a simple acceptance of the story that science had to tell about humans and their faculties—was not enough. This was because they thought that there was a genuine problem about the nature of knowledge, one which could only be resolved by redescribing the known—matter—in a way which was unscientific and specifically philosophical. Thus, in the period prior to Wittgenstein and Ryle, both sides in controversies about the "irreducibility" of the mental agreed that there was *something* mysterious about the mind— something which needed philosophical clarification. They did so because the question "What do we need to know about ourselves which science cannot tell us?" seemed urgent, and because they thought that philosophy, by discovering something about mind, could tell us something about the self-image human beings should have. So both dualists, who invented the mental as successor to the divine, and naturalists, who wanted to de-divinize man without thereby trivializing him, agreed that the blur represented by the concept of "mind" was a suitable topic for philosophical reflection.

On the view I am suggesting, we should just stop being afraid of science and of vulgar materialism. We should substitute the question "What *further* descriptions of ourselves do we need, in addition to those with which science provides us?" for the question "What knowledge of ourselves can theologians or philosophers give us which scientists cannot?" The difference between "description" and "knowledge" is the essence of the matter. To say that the terminology of a materialistic science (and what other kind of science is there?) is unsatisfactory in providing us with a self-image is obviously true. But this does not imply that there is something science does not know, much less something which language cannot capture. It only shows that we need *many different* descriptions of ourselves—some for some purposes and others for others, some for predicting and controlling ourselves and others for deciding what to do, what meaning our lives shall have.[39] There is no need to say that each such description should be grounded on the discovery of a part of our real essence—what we really are deep down inside. Indeed, on the nominalist view I am suggesting, there is no sense to such a claim.

If you accept this pragmatical nominalist outlook, then you will see the attempt of village verificationists like myself to discard the philosophers' blurry concept of mind as essaying the same cultural function as that performed by village atheists who urged that we discard the theologians' blurry concept of God. We are insisting that our moral dignity—our sense of moral obligations and rights, of the uniqueness of our species—is compatible with the ubiquity of scientific explanation, with there being nothing more to discover about ourselves than science has discovered or will discover. We are arguing that our sense of moral worth should not be dependent upon a theological or philosophical account of our real essence. We are urging that the question as to our place in nature has been pretty well settled—that it is highly unlikely that further scientific developments will second-guess Huxley.

But we are also urging that when we have learned our place in nature we have only begun. For beyond the vocabularies useful for prediction and control—the vocabulary of natural science—there are the vocabularies of our moral and our political life and of the arts, of all those human activities which are not aimed at prediction and control but rather in giving us self-images which are worthy of our species. Such images are not true to the nature of species or false to it, for what is really distinctive about us is that we can rise above questions of truth or falsity. We are the poetic species, the one which can change itself by changing its behavior—and especially its linguistic behavior, the words it uses. The ability is not to be explained by discovering more about the nature of something called "the mind" any more than by discovering more about the nature of something called "God." Such attempts to "ground" our ability to recreate ourselves by seeking its ineffable source are, in Sartre's sense, self-deceptive. They are attempts to find a vocabulary, a way of speaking, which will be more than *just* a way of speaking. To say, with nominalism, that language is ubiquitous and to deny, with verificationism, that there are intuitions to which our language must conform, is just to assert that we need nothing more than confidence in our own poetic power.

RORTY: *Conversations*

WHEELER: It is wonderful to hear this account in which one sees in one sense the mind is not magic, and in another sense it is magic, and it reminds one of the question one asks his friends among the biologists—is mind unique? One learns from his biological friends that any creature, small or large, has to seek food. To seek food, it has to have a sensor. This sensor may be simple, as it is in the simplest creatures, or complicated, as it is in the most complicated. But it's also so interesting to discover, as I learn from Ernst Mayr, that the eye, as the highest form of sensory organ, has developed forty times independently in the history of evolution. If we regard the eye as the window of the soul, or the mind, it is inspiring to think that there is an evolutionary force driving the development of this mind which is going to produce it, hell or high water. But still, above all that, there is this higher question—and this, as I understood it from Professor Rorty, also came in because on the one hand the evolutionary point of view was central to his account, but on the other there is the point of poetic language, and I wanted to inquire if this inspiring description of man as the poetic species has ever been used before, because to my mind it is something we would all like to use "in the future."

RORTY: I think this description of human beings is what we got from the Romantic Movement of the turn of the eighteenth century. That is, I think the romantic poets were the people who redescribed man in terms that were neither scientific nor theological—terms which tried to make the poet rather than the knower the paradigmatic human being. I am simply lifting these notions from the Romantics. But I think that the comparison between an evolutionary force, working toward the creation of something, and the human imaginative drive toward the poetic is misleading. What was interesting about Darwinian accounts was that they didn't have to use the notion of an evolutionary drive. By *mechanizing* the evolutionary process they permitted us to say that one can be romantic in our attitude toward man without requiring that science provide confirmation for romanticism.

PANNENBERG: I cannot fully agree with Professor Rorty, because we should not sacrifice a phenomenon like the "intuition of mind." The same as with living beings—the fact that there are living beings around is a phenomenon to be explained and the question is whether scientific methods, physicalism—in the way we have it today—is sufficient to explain it in terms of physical theory. But I think we have to start with the fact that there are living beings around—that's a phenomenon of life, and science is to explain the phenomenon. The same is true, I feel, with the question of minds, and as soon as I am offered a theory that does away with the phenomenon . . . I'm somewhat puzzled.

RORTY: I do want to disagree with Professor Pannenberg on the question of whether these are facts to be explained. It may seem weird to say that there might turn out to be no living bodies, or that there might turn out to be no minds. It was of course weird to say it turned out that the earth was not at rest. It seems to me that what we need to explain is not the truth of a proposition, but the inclination of human beings to assert the proposition. The Copernican theory enables us to explain why everybody instantly assents to the proposition "the earth stands still," even though it does so on the basis of the earth's movement. What we need to explain is the popularity of our present speech habits, which classify things as living, nonliving, cognitive, noncognitive, morally relevant, morally irrelevant. Our explanation may or may not preserve those propositions; but, in my view, a phenomenon is merely our inclination to assent to certain propositions. That inclination, if you like, is the phenomenon that has to be explained. But the explanation need not be in terms of the truth of the propostions we are inclined to believe. Though, of course, most of the time it will be, because science, like any sensible human activity, is instinctively conservative.

PANNENBERG: I would like to take issue with the sentence that the phenomenon is to be explained in terms of the inclinations of people. This is a very strong hypothesis, to say the least. There is a difference between finding something and producing something at will. There is a difference, and this difference is what I think is important. I do not agree that the term "mind" would be a creation of idealistic philosophy, especially in the modern period of time. That is not true. Of course Professor Rorty knows that, that the term mind translates the Latin term *mens*, and certainly we have to admit that there is not a precise equivalent to *mens* in other ancient languages. But even to be able to make such a translation presupposes that there was an understanding, that in spite of the differences of language, there's some same phenomena involved that people were trying to talk about. So, it's not an invention of idealistic philosophy, although it is of course rooted in the relativities of history, of the aristocracy of human experience, of the history of human language. Still, in human language we find something, naming it. Our perspectives may change, but that doesn't substantially replace that model that we find something which has to be explained. It is not a theory. The term mind, as such, is not a theory. There are a lot of theories about the mind, but the term mind is not a theory. It gives expression to human experience as condensed in language.

RORTY: My disagreements with Professor Pannenberg here are so radical that I'm afraid that I am going to sound merely dogmatic. His closing phrase about the notion of experience condensed in language seems to me to convey precisely the image of the relation between language and the rest of human capacities which is central to the philosophical tradition. I admit that it sounds wildly paradoxical to say that what is given for explanation is our assent to sentences rather than what we find in the word. But I think that it is extremely helpful to think of scientific explanation in those terms. I wish that Sir Karl Popper were here, because this would be the one point in my paper he might actually agree with. The positivistic account of scientific explanation makes a central theme of the claim that what science is to explain are propositions; that the test of an explanation is testing one sentence's ability to stand in certain inferential relationships with other sentences. For all its faults, positivism's contribution to the philosophy of science was to emphasize that understanding explanation is understanding a linguistic phenomena, not a relation between language and something else (e.g., experience) which is condensed in language. But this is an enormously long story within the philosophy of science which I shouldn't try to relate.

AUDIENCE: . . .Weisenbaum, in his book *Computer Power and Human Reason,* argues that even if computers gain the ability to perform tasks which, if performed by a human being, would be called intelligent, they should not be allowed to perform these tasks if these tasks pit machines against men. For example, computers should not become jurists, judges, or therapists even if that were possible. Presumably, it's the question of human dignity. How would you feel about being judged by a jury of machines, albeit competent?

RORTY: That seems much like the question posed in the nineteenth century, "How would you feel about being judged by a jury of women?" The audience in the nineteenth century would have felt very strange. We would feel very strange being judged by a jury of computers. I haven't the slightest idea whether it would be a good idea to use computers on juries. At the moment it's a moot point, because computers are still sufficiently stupid that no one has any intention of so using them. If, in the future, computers become what the artificial intelligence freaks tell us they will become, then it will be, I suppose, a serious question whether to use them on juries. But I don't think it will have anything to do with human dignity. That is, either computers will become part of a moral community in the way in which blacks, women, and so on became part of a moral community, or they won't. But there is not going to be any nice neat philosophical answer to the question whether they should or not, any more than there was a nice neat philosophical answer to the question whether blacks and women should.

ELVEE: Professor Wigner.

WIGNER: I think science's function is to describe certain phenomena in a simple and interesting way. Now, the question which most of us physicists feel in connection with mind is, "Do you think that present-day science could be extended to this phenomenon or whether there will be, again, some fundamental changes needed in our science to encompass the phenomenon of mind?" Can you answer this question?

RORTY: Well, my own hunch would be that there are phenomena currently so little understood—not so much psychological as biological phenomena—as to suggest that the present vocabulary of the physical sciences may not be adequate. This is the merest hunch. My inclination, however, is to say that these mysteries turn up not in the higher human powers—not in the mental particularly—but in much more basic activities of living organisms. That's again just a hunch. So . . . I wouldn't be quite happy with there being deep ontological mysteries about life any more than with mind, but I'm a little happier about life than about mind.

WIGNER: Of course, most physicists believe that there is a continuous transition between no-life and life just as there is a continuous transition between the situation in which only gravitational forces play a role and the situation in which electromagnetic forces play a tremendously important role, and we believe that science is similar. That perhaps present-day physics can describe the behavior and life of bacteria, but not that of a dog. Is that reasonable? Perhaps.

RORTY: Well, I'm not sure what to say in reply to that. I'm inclined to say that it all depends on what you want to know about the dog. It seems to me that there's an awful lot about the dog that we can explain pretty well. I am more troubled by the migration of butterflies than I am by anything that dogs do. So it isn't the gap between the bacteria and the dog that bothers me particularly, any more than the gap between the dog and the scientific genius. I don't think that these, as it were, stages in complexity are the places where something fundamental might have to be done. I think it may be odd incidental little phenomena that aren't captured by the usual philosophical picture of the great chain of being that might be the really difficult cases.

ELVEE: Professor Wheeler deferred comment on the implications of physics on questions about the nature of the mind on the ground that a philosopher should speak about this. But Professor Rorty seems to be passing the buck back to the physicists. What are the consequences of the claim that a phenomenon does not exist until it is recorded for the existence of mind? Does it not suggest that the mind exists independently of physical nature and influences it?

RORTY: I think perhaps the best way to answer that would be by reverting to the analogy between the mind and God. It seems to me the nineteenth century was full of bad questions of the form, "Does this latest thing that the scientists tell us cause us to have less faith in God, more faith in God, this kind of doubt about God, that kind of doubt about God . . . ?" It seems to me that the theological tradition which insists that whatever science comes up with won't really matter to our relationship with God, is right. This because God is not an explanatory notion. He shouldn't be used in an explanatory role. The same thing seems to me to hold for the notion of mind. As the term is used in daily life (in phrases like, "Jones doesn't know his own mind, Smith is out of his mind"), there is nothing wrong with the notion. As it is used in the philosophical tradition, it seems to me, it is a notion which we should just not bother about any more. So we shouldn't try to answer questions like, "What are the implications of this or that scientific development for mind?"

NOTES

1. Thomas H. Huxley, *Man's Place in Nature* (Ann Arbor: University of Michigan Press, 1959). This essay was originally published in 1863 under the title "Evidence as to Man's Place in Nature."

2. C. D. Broad, *The Mind and Its Place in Nature* (New York: Humanities Press, 1951).
3. Gilbert Ryle, *The Concept of Mind* (London: Hutchinson, 1949).
4. Daniel Dennett, *Brainstorms* (Montgomery, Vermont: Bradford Books, 1978).
5. Broad, *The Mind and Its Place in Nature*, p. 613.
6. Ibid., p. 614.
7. Thomas Nagel, *Mortal Questions* (Cambridge: Cambridge University Press, 1979), p. 188.
8. Ibid., p. 177.
9. Arthur O. Lovejoy, *The Revolt Against Dualism* (La Salle, Illinois: Open Court Publishing Company, 1930), p. 1.
10. Ibid., p. 3.
11. Ibid., p. 13.
12. Ibid., pp. 14–15.
13. Ryle, *The Concept of Mind*, p. 155.
14. Ibid., p. 158.
15. Ibid., p. 159.
16. Ibid., p. 169. Karl Popper points out this tension in Ryle's thought in Karl C. Popper and John C. Eccles, *The Self and Its Brain* (Berlin: Springer, 1977), pp. 105–6.
17. I was guilty of this sort of mistake myself in various papers which I published in the period of 1965–71. I tried to do better by distinguishing various ingredients in our blurry concept of "the mental" in Chapter 1 of *Philosophy and the Mirror of Nature* (Princeton: Princeton University Press, 1979). For the views of Smart and Putnam, see their articles, respectively titled "Sensations and Brain Processes" and "The Nature of Mental States," in David M. Rosenthal, ed., *Materialism and the Mind-Body Problem* (Englewood Cliffs, New Jersey: Prentice-Hall, 1971).
18. Hilary Putnam, *Reason, Truth and History* (Cambridge: Cambridge University Press, 1981), p. 81.
19. Dennett, *Brainstorms*, pp. 152–153.
20. Ibid., p. 154.
21. John R. Searle, "Minds, Brains and Programs" in *The Behavioral and Brain Sciences* 3 (1980), p. 422.
22. Ibid., pp. 419–20.
23. Ibid., p. 420. This claim is central to many of Searle's arguments against a Sellarsian account of awareness as a "linguistic affair" and thus against a functionalist account of cognition. For by insisting that no account of thought will do which deprives non-language-using animals (e.g., dogs) of thoughts, he insists that we preserve precisely the concept of thought which Dennett thinks incoherent. (See Dennett, *Brainstorms*, p. 38, and chapter 2 passim.) Searle's forthcoming book on the philosophy of mind turns around the claim that any analysis must cover dogs and men, a claim which presupposes that our use of the term "thought" in ordinary language expresses an intuition which any psychological or philosophi-

cal account must preserve. This strategy seems to me to preserve the bad, "ordinary language philosophy" side of Ryle—the portion of Ryle's work which the development of central-state materialism and functionalism helped us to set aside.

24. Nagel, *Mortal Questions*, p. 174.

25. Ibid., p. 174. Here Nagel takes for granted that one can analyze the notion of "appearance" only in terms of presentation to consciousness, rather than (in the manner of Sellars) in terms of the use of a certain sort of statement (one containing locutions like "seems"). For the latter analysis, see Wilfrid Sellars, *Science, Perception and Reality* (London: Routledge Kegan Paul, 1963), pp. 140–156.

26. This position is sometimes criticized as "instrumentalist," but that is a misleading term. The nominalist is not saying that science cannot find out what is really there, but rather that "really there" (*both* for the referents of the perceptual vocabulary of common sense and those of the theoretical vocabularies of science) means nothing more than "what we find it most useful to talk about."

27. Dennett, *Brainstorms*, p. xiv.

28. Nagel, *Mortal Questions*, p. 166.

29. Ibid., p. 171.

30. Ibid., p. 171.

31. Dennett, *Brainstorms*, p. 173.

32. Ibid., p. 168.

33. Ibid.

34. Ibid., pp. 168–69.

35. The phrase comes from Ludwig Wittgenstein, *Philosophical Investigations* (London: Macmillan, 1953), Part I, section 271.

36. Searle, "Minds, Brains and Programs," p. 420.

37. See *Philosophy and the Mirror of Nature*, chapter 4, and the Introduction to my forthcoming *Consequences of Pragmatism* (Minneapolis: University of Minnesota Press, 1982).

38. Thus when Nagel says that "there are facts which do not consist in the truth of propositions expressible in a human language" (Nagel, *Mortal Questions*, p. 171) I see his view as the contemporary expression of William James's admiration for the mystic, the person who has experiences such that "no adequate report of its content can be given in words" (William James, *Varieties of Religious Experience* [New York: Longmans, 1902], p. 380.) Wittgenstein, who read James's book and repeated James's point about "das Mystische" in terms of what lies "beyond the limits of language," seems to me the genealogical link between James and Nagel. (See Ludwig Wittgenstien, *Tractatus Logico-Philosophicus* [London: Kegan Paul, 1922], 6.522.) I am grateful to Marx Wartofsky for reminding me of Feuerbach's remark that *Geist* is a successor concept of God.

39. I develop this point at greater length in "Method, Social Science and Social Hope" included in *Consequences of Pragmatism*.

Reflections on the Evolution of The Mind and Its Environment

RAGNAR GRANIT

"Un seul pouvoir governera rééllement le
monde, ce sera la science, ce sera l'esprit."
ERNEST RENAN , *Dialogues philosophiques.**

I. The Biological Approach

Introduction

In defining the theme of this conference, the College has
given us a generous option. With the whole of our civilization
created by the conscious activity of the human mind, we
would seem to be free to choose among a wide variety of
approaches to the subject. Mine will be that of a physiologist
interested in information, action, and control of the operations of the nervous system.

In the present age my science, which used to be almost
exclusively devoted to the study of specific physico-chemical
mechanisms in the body, has been forced by its own technical
progress to take a serious interest in problems of the type I
mentioned. Many of them are of the kind that concern interaction between an organism and its environment and so
mind—or conscious registration of information, voluntary
action, and exercise of control—has come closer to our central issues. These, as always, are experimental and nowadays

---

* "Knowledge and Spirit, these alone govern the world."—Renan

largely—though by no means exclusively—based on micro-electrodes and electronics. While probing various sites in the nervous system with our electrodes, we are allowed glimpses of mind in the making or in action—that is, we can trace tracks of mind in fragments of perception and in the executive apparatus obeying commands of our will.

Evolutionary Aspects

Like so many other biologists, I think of mind or conscious awareness as an emergent property in the evolution of life. This implies that it exists *in nuce* in properties of matter, just as does the insulin molecule or the double helix containing DNA. The chemist will tell us that such organizations of matter are fully explicable by laws governing the formation of the chemical bonds. I have no reason to distrust them on that point; but when they assert that emergent properties in new organizations of matter are fully understood from the fact that they do not violate any chemical laws, I find their conclusion indefensible. There is in hierarchic biological systems a creative resourcefulness for which a typical fragmentary analysis in a science such as chemistry has not the necessary arsenal of concepts. In fact, it is a major deficiency in present-day science that the creative language based on structural reorganizations is spoken above its head. Emergent novelties have to be accepted as such, though sometimes compressible into a chemical formula. One can state with Heisenberg about living organisms "dass sie, wenn man sie als Maschinen behandelt, sich auch wie Maschinen verhalten wurden."[1*]

By analogy, the role of a structure, such as the manmade computer, simple by comparison with our brain, cannot be understood from the laws governing the instrumentation of its hardware. With mind, it shares a control function dependent on a specific organization of its components. This con-

---

* "That they, if one treats them like machines, would also behave like machines."—Heisenberg

trol function is inserted into the design of the computer by a mind which itself has evolved in a struggle for, so to speak, a double control, firstly of the nervous system, secondly of the environment. In the evolutionary process of selection, both types of control must have had survival value.

William James adumbrated the first function when he wrote: "The distribution of consciousness shows it to be exactly such as we might expect in an organ added for the sake of steering a nervous system grown too complex to regulate itself."[2] Such self-control would also have been a *conditio sine qua non* for survival of the organism in relation to the environment, and so these two aspects of conscious control give mind its place in nature, as it emerges in evolution. The value of possessing conscious awareness in relation to the environment is easily appreciated, but the basic questions of mind and brain turn around cellular complexity and self-control, as James apparently understood. I shall make an attempt at following up this line of thought.

In order to illustrate what cellular complexity really looks like in relation to mind, let me choose the voluntary motor act which implicates mind and muscles in speech or movement. *Will* is a psychological entity enclosing the purpose of the motor activity. It rules over a complex executive power supply in muscles whose entries and exits in action have to be precisely steered for timing, acceleration, strength, and duration of their individual activities. For this there is a hierarchy of control upon control, upon control, etc. Working upwards from below there are in the periphery the end plates of nerves on muscles, next the motoneurons in the spinal cord, their segmental surrounding interneurons, the special gamma motoneurons adjusting the sensitivity of the sensory endings called muscle spindles, the so-called basal ganglia of the brain, the cerebellum, the thalamus, and the cerebral sensory-motor cortex that acts directly and indirectly on the motoneurons. Electrical records from these sites—in cats, monkeys, and partly, also in man—have shown them to cooperate in limb movements of the kind that at least in monkeys already can be intentional.[3] My favorite example has been the organist whose range of coordinated movements extends over three keyboards and pedals, when he is reading a score that also has to be made musically palatable. His movements in space are extensive enough to require continuous postural compensations to prevent him falling from his chair. Automatic reflex controls of posture are integrated into the movements, mobilizing subsystems based on information from many afferent sources, in particular from muscles and from vestibularis, the balance organs in the ears.

In voluntary movement our mind handles complex nervous operations in a dictatorial fashion. Instant obedience is required for any changing aim of action. Obstacles must be overcome. Thus we can write with a pencil tied to a shaft lengthening our arm, or even with one inserted between the toes. In voluntary acts the will is tied to the purpose. To this everything must be subordinated. Mind, the psychological dictator, rules by order-giving and pays no attention to the chemical machinery employed. It has supreme control. Evolution has put a premium on the development of intended action in living beings. Mind in purposive voluntary activity represents its present summit.

Most people are likely to think of mind in connection with sensory awareness of a perceived world rather than with motor activity, but Sherrington, who was one of the most experienced neurobiologists of our time, held the view that mind had evolved as an aid to motoricity.[4] The automatic reflex is the predecessor of the voluntary motor act, and it still lies in our power to automatize movements that began as an emanation of will.

In order to understand how mind has invaded the sensory end of the original reflex, let us begin by taking our imagination to the period in evolution when a lens had been created across a photosensitive indentation in the skin. This implied a distortion of the image dependent on the distance of the projected object. To counteract the false information, the nervous system was compelled to develop corrective processes which, at our stage of the evolution, in the mind's eye appear as relative constancies of the size of objects in our environment. When moving about, we move in the mentally corrected world of sight, and so must animals have done at evolutionary stages virtually devoid of conscious action. But the mind has been quick to recognize size constancy as a psychological fact. To put this in the words of Mayr, "the ever ready opportunism of evolution"[5] has been at work!

Another example of mind entering into fairly well-known sensory developments: it begins with the ciliary hairs in the lateral line of primitive fish using them to sense vibrations and the direction of currents streaming through or perhaps even past the line organ. The land animals have transformed this structure, that at the level of the reptiles is evolution's first attempt at producing an ear, into such an organ, a development completed in the mammals. Every stage in these comprehensive transformations has been traced by the anatomists. Step by step the original cilia and the canal have been adapted to aid hearing and the vestibular senses, retaining their fundamental role of serving as mechano-receptors. It would take us too far to recapitulate these changes in detail.[6] In the present context, it is one more illustration of the "opportunism" of Mayr's that characterizes evolutionary creativity. Ultimately, conscious awareness is grafted upon these transformations of the sense organ and reaches its climax in musicality. This great invention has presupposed a corresponding creative development of the central nervous system to match the peripheral sensory adaptation from water life to land life.

Role of Cell Number

Is there any way of closing in on the background of conscious mind in localization, structural detail, requirements of any kind, beyond stating that consciousness presupposes a living brain? Some limiting conditions have been summarized by Doty.[7] As to localization of consciousness Penfield held the view that it depended on, or was localized to, a "centrencephalic centre" in the midbrain.[8] Doty reviews the experimental criticism of Penfield's hypothesis and accepts it as conclusive. The general standpoint in this matter again is Sherrington's, namely, that consciousness requires the "roof brain" (the cortex) and, indeed, as he pointed out has developed in parallel with the expansion of the cerebral cortex.[9]

The work of Sperry and his colleagues,[10] that has led to a differentiation of the contribution to conscious awareness of the two hemispheres after section of the cerebral commissures, can hardly be understood without accepting the conclusion that consciousness depends on the "roof brain." Besides, as Doty pointed out, in some split-brain patients the centrencephalic system is intact and yet incapable of producing the integrated bihemispheric mind. This integrated mind requires the impulses in the two hundred million fibers of the corpus callosum joining right and left hemisphere. Put in another way, this ties consciousness to an exchange of information mediated by these nervous impulses, the most definite piece of knowledge on its localization so far obtainable. Another valuable observation follows from the studies of blood distribution, as initiated by Ingvar and Lassen, [11] Ingvar in particular interesting himself in psychologically defined acts and states.[12] It seems that mentation especially engages the frontal lobes.

A number of arguments can be adduced to support the conclusion that consciousness is *the* essential multicellular process, in the sense that it requires activation of an extraordinary quantity of cellular material. Today this is not as self-evident as it may have appeared to James when he considered the complexity of the brain. The study of single cortical cells by microelectrodes has shown them to respond to repeatable combinations of natural stimuli in a highly specific manner. In some tests they behave like small "homunculi" in selecting specifications. This is so characteristic that it has led to the extravagant suggestion that each familiar face is memorized in a special cell. Yet so far no one has produced evidence for a type of cell representing consciousness! The closest approach to it, in terms of the microelectrode technique, is the observation by Mountcastle and his group that certain cells in the parietal area which respond to a foveal target within reach of the monkey's arm, do so only if the target interests the animal.[13] The step from "interest" to conscious awareness is likely to be short. But then, how many cells are mobilized for something defined as "interest"?

My own line of thought has been that conscious awareness arises from a highly *multicellular organizational pattern*, best developed in man. Its design remains unknown and so, for the moment, we can only consider arguments relating James's complexity to cell number. The intricate synaptic connectivity, as implied in cell number as a general concept, need not at the present stage of our knowledge be brought up.

A commonplace observation is that learning to execute a complex movement under conscious control requires a large expenditure of energy because in the beginning muscles participate that in the end are unnecessary, and those needed still act uneconomically. Our final aim is to automatize as much of the movement as possible. A cortical counterpart to this experience is a finding of the physiologists training dogs for conditional reflexes under elecroencephalographic control. Before the dog has learned to handle the problem facing him, the electrical activity accompanying the effort is spread over large portions of the brain. In the fully trained animal, the active site has shrunk to a small focus responding to the challenge. The learned behavior is then fully automatized and the voluntary effort is restricted to a trigger function. Clearly this finding is in good agreement with the hypothesis that conscious activity is a highly multicellular event. Once achievment of its goal has been automatized and deposited in memory, cell number is reduced to the necessary minimum.

Cell number may be taken as the common denominator of several observations related to consciousness. Thus Sherrington's view that consciousness increased with the expansion of the roof brain recurs in a modernized form as the magnitude of the "encephalization factor." This factor is a kind of general size index of the brain of each species serving to neutralize the effect of variable body weight in the comparison of different species. Man has the highest encephalization factor of all animals, thirty as against ten for the next of kin, the great apes.[14] The total cerebral cortical area of man is 3.5 times greater than that of the orangutan, but within that figure is concealed the finding that the frontal lobes in man occupy an area 6.3 times greater than that of the orangutan.[15] Now the frontal lobes, as pointed out above, are particularly active in mentation, to judge by the blood distribution (Ingvar).

Several observations can be adduced to prove that highgrade performance, optimally controlled, requires cellular expansion at the cortical level. Thus the hand and face areas are enormous compared with those representing the rest of the body, [16]as is true for both motor and sensory spheres. Closing my eyes, I think I even feel a kind of awareness of the existence of hands and face whereas the back appears dead silent. Our little pinpoint fovea, responsible for most of our conscious seeing, is 10,000 times expanded in the primary visual area[17] and, in addition, specifically represented at several cortical sights of a higher order.[18] At the retina, by contrast, peripheral vision, dominated by a nonanalytic detector function, occupies an enormous field compared with that of the fovea. The important interhemispheric callosal connections are also restricted to the fovea.

In conclusion, then, the most definite statement a physiologist can make about conscious awareness is that it is organized by an exceedingly large number of cells, is normally bihemispherically integrated, and presupposes a living brain. The latter condition implies energy consumption. Horton Johnson has pointed out that the brain comes next to the liver in energy consumption.[19] This is maintenance cost, like the energy in the vacuum tube of the old radio receivers heated for performance. The human brain permanently consumes about 14 watts of power. "The additional cost of conscious information processing or wakeful thought is trivial by comparison." But then, of course, Johnson, stating this, has not looked at the pictures of shifts in blood distribution that illustrate different types of psychic activity.[20] These local needs must not be averaged away.

When Brodal points out that "the anatomical possibilities for (more or less) direct cooperation between various parts of the brain must be almost unlimited,"[21] it really is mind alone that instantaneously is capable of availing itself of these unlimited interconnections. This it does in a fluctuating synthetic awareness of the sensori-motor actuality, as it changes from moment to moment taking memory into account. Conscious awareness is a unifying process in the sense that it, as William James said, "does not appear to itself chopped up in bits."[22] Impressions from different sensory spheres may coexist with an emotional tint based on present and past experience. At the same time, as we shall see, the mind is capable of analyzing its experiences by subdividing them. Memory and emotional inheritance blend in giving each mind its individual character.

The popularization of the work on so-called split-brain patients may have led some to question the notion of an all-embracing single mind. However, James with uncanny foresight anticipated Sperry's[23] findings in this field when he pointed out that there are persons whose "total possible consciousness may be split into parts which coexist but naturally ignore each other." This is precisely what is seen in the split-brain patients when the two halves are kept apart by experimental screening of their individual inputs. The differential localization of function to the right and left hemispheres does not bother our mind.

Those who have followed me this far may well ask whether there is any likelihood for computers ever to develop consciousness? My answer is: none whatever! Part of what the mind stands for can undoubtedly be represented by computer logic. It is, after all, an extension of a corresponding component of our conscious processes, as translated by speech and mathematics. But our mind has other sources of inspiration that cannot be formulated within the realm of any imitable logic complexity. Conscious man is aware of feelings, love, hatred, admiration, respect, he is consciously sensitive to beauty, ugliness, tristesse, grandeur. He is musical, and he can read between the lines of the verbal art of poetry. Our mind is also curiously sensitive to mass psychoses, and somehow I can only take it as a major joke to visualize some hundred manlike computers taking part in a demonstration outside an embassy!

II. Mind and Environment

The creative force in evolution is held to be natural selection weeding out destructive mutations so that useful ones can be multiplied by the differential reproduction thus made possible. The survival value of mind in this process is difficult to define with the precision that sometimes can be reached in experiments on insects and bacteria and perhaps also in population genetics. We have to be content with James's answer, discussed above, and with a notion as general as that of control of the environment. The numerous aspects of this notion cannot be taken up here. For us, mind simply is there to be accepted. Its assets I have discussed elsewhere.[24]

From the point of view of mind and environment, a question of greater interest is whether conscious awareness has implied a big enough innovation to have become the most important force in the evolution of mankind today. I believe this to be the case and will now try to motivate my thesis.

At a rather early stage in the evolution of mammals, sensory reproduction of the external world as well as a number of intentional acts must have been established. But the major step that man took with growing consciousness, and one that also promoted it, was creation of communication by speech, now known to be a universal characteristic of all humanity. It implied symbolizing reality in terms of variable sounds, syllables, substantives, verbs, adjectives, and inventing rules for transforming an internal semantic structure into sentences of grammatic correctness. Dubos has rightly emphasized that man, symbolizing everything that happens to him, then reacts "to the symbols as if they were actual environmental stimuli."[25]

By this trait, man has freed himself from the need of personal experience for backing up knowledge of things, relations, happenings, emotions while still able to share them with his fellow beings. The society of communication thus established has originated the joint efforts required for its manifold purposes. Symbolizing or labeling fragments of conscious experience as in speech seems to me a peculiar and spectacular achievement of a mind that is undivisible and which cannot be "chopped up in bits." It, so to speak, does the chopping itself.

I can understand its capacity for fragmentation of experience only when considering that conscious awareness operates physiologically by scanning and briefly focusing on sites in a cortex that we know represents differential localization of functions. At every instant its content is changeable but limited. The eye movements consisting of saccades and drifts behave in the same way. The effect of this characteristic of mind will be the old Roman rule: *divide et impera!*

Analysis by fragmentation has reached its summit in the natural sciences. The particles and waves of physics, the chemists' formulas, the single cell, its mitochondria, the isolated nervous impulse, the Boolean algebra are all examples of this property of mind. Experience is fragmented until in the end the result is a world of symbols and causalities nonexistent to the so-called five senses. However, this is nevertheless a real world in its own right, because it stands for the language of applicability as spoken by our technology.

Entering the empire of technology means returning to an aspect of consciousness that I briefly mentioned in the beginning of my talk, that of volition. Many writers discussing mind and matter wholly neglect its component of action, which is so important when considering the place of mind in nature and its role in evolution. The scientific world of knowledge would be of largely academic interest—a delightful piece of creation—if it were not for the will to use it for practical purposes. This brings us back to consider voluntary activity as such and in relation to the environment.

The will is neither more nor less of a riddle than sensory awareness of the environment and cognition. Awareness of intent in speech and other voluntary motor activities is in fact so important that motor acts without intent and purpose generally are held to be a sign of mental disease. Thus the drive in voluntary activity, be it speech, manipulation of objects, or locomotion, derives from the purpose or goal that is being anticipated. To this its execution in motoricity is wholly subordinated, though important in its own right for adequate performance. The mind may be described as inventor of purpose and dictator of action when from its motor apparatus it is requesting means for realizing its fancy. This is of course highly pertinent to its place in nature. Purposive conscious acts represent a new factor in the evolution of man himself and of the environment in which he is living.

Evolutionary theory does not accept purposiveness. It holds the view that evolution, in being "directive," is directed by chance and natural selection in populations fit to reproduce. Man is merely a piece in this gigantic game of Nature's. But this same man is also a conscious being whose purposive activity is steered by rational considerations towards goals he himself has found necessary or attractive. He may decide to take the evolution of his species in his own hands, thereby interfering with Nature's balance sheet. His criteria for survival value have very little in common with those that have prevailed during earlier stages in the evolutionary game of chance and natural selection—assuming neo-Darwinistic theory to be correct.

These facts and reflections are the basis for my conclusion that mind is a significant enough innovation to alter the course of evolution by its goal-directed voluntary activity.

Evolutionary theory would, by acknowledging the reality of the emanations of will from living minds, come closer to the factor analysis of causes that it is trying to establish.

Man is conceited enough to hold for his own prerogative what is called "will." But on the view that I have adopted here, will is an evolutionary product growing in significance in the scale of animal species, as does the conscious awareness of which it is the active component. Mind's influence on evolution may well have preceded its own final perfection in man.

The picture I have painted of the place of mind in nature, as considered from the standpoint of a biologist, would—I believe—find acceptance by the majority of my colleagues interested in these problems, even when they would want to add a great deal out of their own heads and present the matter differently. It is based on the synthetic theory of evolution, but at the same time tries to find a place for the development of the human mind, master of communication and dictator of action, no greater invention in evolutionary history. We know that every environmental influence to which a species is exposed over a sufficiently long time in the end will be reflected in its genetic makeup. The creative activities of mind can hardly claim to be exceptions. In fact, if we had proper methods available for measuring their influence it would hardly come as a surprise to discover that it already exists.

I feel it would be a mistake wholly to neglect other attitudes to the phenomenon Mind than the biological one presented here. Probably most people think of it in religious terms, as does, for instance, my old colleague and friend J. C. Eccles,[26] a great leader in neurophysiology. But from his standpoint a still greater independence would be ascribed to mind.

All scientists are not willing to attribute to chance the dominant role it has in the synthetic theory of evolution. Einstein is often quoted for his opinion that "God does not play dice." This utterance may have been inspired by the probabilistic quantum-theoretical explanations that Heisenberg arrived at when working out his uncertainty rule. But Einstein's criticism would apply equally to the chance supposed to be responsible for mutations with subsequent gene flow and recombination. It would imply that the observed genetic variations by mutation obey secret laws, as yet undiscovered. While keeping an open mind on this point, I still maintain that replacement of chance by unknown natural laws does not alter the gist of my conclusions as to the place of mind in nature.

Divine interference, chance plus natural selection, or an evolution liberated from the element of chance, all tend to raise the question of the kind of goal humanity is heading for. Will it be Ragnarrok, the catastrophe prophesied in the Nordic myths, or that of the great French humanist Ernest Renan: "le but du monde est la production d'une conscience reflechie de plus en plus perfectionne."[27] The alternatives are legion and theoretically our choice among them is free.

The resources of our mind have not yet been fully explored and pedagogy is still an art and not a science. As a matter of fact we live so intensely in our conscious world of imagination with its plans, hopes and resentments, nourished by memory, that for us the real world mostly is less real than its imaginary opposite in each individual consciousness. Instead of considering mind's place in nature, we as individuals are concerned with nature's place in mind. This aspect is also what we are studying in experimental physiology. With me the results of such work have led to questioning the claims of fragmentary natural science when they exceed what can be proved, as I said in my introduction. This followed from my preoccupation with neurophysiology in its sensory and motor aspects. It was obvious that the interaction of mind with the environment could not be understood without accepting the purposiveness of voluntary action, a clearly antiphysical notion. In the experimental work of today, it recurs under the protective screen of the term "plastic adaptability."

GRANIT: *Conversations*

WIGNER: Some people, and I'm afraid I agree with them, think that natural selection could not have produced, even over the long time period available, as complex and as well-functioning organisms as those of animals and man. This is a little different from what you said.

GRANIT: Well, what should I say. Even today people can produce an insulin molecule at a moment's notice by a recombination in the E-coli bacteria, so that with that event, I have seen tremendous changes in no time. And what nature has been up to is something that we only can guess at. But I see no impossibility in that. You can introduce a new factor in a simple way by heating a banana fly. If the eggs are heated at forty degrees, after awhile you get generations of banana flies with streaks on the wings and they last a long, long time. Gradually, on returning to normal hatching temperature, they are weeded out—a change, a mutation disappearing. I don't think that one should think of mutation rate as being so very slow. We have even now started our own mutations.

WIGNER: I have one more remark, if you forgive me, and that is that the only point on which I can't entirely agree with Professor Granit is that it is impossible to create life materially. I think that it is entirely possible that, if we make sufficient complications, life can be created. I have two points of evidence for that. The first one is that bacteria probably have very little true life and therefore, if we made a system which is chemically and physically very similar to those of bacteria, probably they would assume life. Is that reasonable? My second argument is that even though ordinary bodies have no electricity, if I hook two together, I can create electricity, so that the creation of something new is not excluded just because the original substance doesn't contain it.

GRANIT: You are coming into genetics again, and I appeal to Professor Snell to give the answer.*

SNELL: I am not one of the speakers here, so I feel a little out of place. But on this subject I was brought up as a geneticist and a student of evolution, and I do puzzle over the question [of] whether, to explain the evolution of man, you have to bring in some force

---

* George D. Snell, winner of the Nobel Prize in Physiology and Medicine in 1980 and guest of the conference.

beyond that which the evolutionist and the statistician and the geneticist have postulated. Frankly, I can't really convince myself that it's necessary—although certainly, when you reach the level of complexity of man, it is perhaps a little difficult to appreciate that the forces of natural selection and mutation can really account for it all. But I cannot convince myself that anything else is necessary, [other] than the basic mechanisms that Darwin postulated.

PANNENBERG: Professor Granit, you agreed, if I understood correctly, in many basic points with the influential publications on the question of mind of Sir John Eccles. He also emphasized the thesis that mind is to be understood as an emerging novelty of evolution, as you said.

GRANIT: All biologists do that!

PANNENBERG: But he emphasizes the point of novelty so that it is not reducible to more primitive forms. Then he also emphasizes that there is an advantage of mind, and especially of language as closely related to mind, in terms of natural selection. So that he even conjectures that the development of the brain in the present form would presuppose the invention of language. I don't know whether you would agree with that point. My question relates more particularly to the dualist position Eccles derives from that. I understood that you would be more hesitant in taking such a dualist position. Would you comment a little more on this question? What is it that divides your position from the interpretation given by Eccles to the many statements you have in common with Eccles?

GRANIT: There are many points in common between us, because we are both neurophysiologists and we have the same starting point, but of course as regards dualism there is still the problem of Jean Fernel of the sixteenth century who said that the soul enters the embryo on the fortieth day of conception. I don't see how dualists can overcome this dilemma. I think, as I said in the beginning, that we don't understand the nature of organization. The analogy of course is the ordinary computer. There are effects that are not in the hardware, but are in the logic of the system. So, I think, inside the brain we have an organizational system that is available to the brain for its control and actions. You speak of the geneticists. They have not, either, really come to the point of what organization might have done in the course of evolution. As soon as there is a new center of organization, it is in its turn creative. That is a missing link in the studies of people and population genetics, as well as in all this material work which is exciting in itself.

PANNENBERG: However, Eccles feels himself driven to the dualist position because, as I understood him, he sees no instance in the brain machinery itself to provide the final integration of the operations going on in the brain.

GRANIT: You may have to wait some time for that!

PANNENBERG: But I would like to have some comment from your side on how you think you avoid what Eccles feels drives him to that position.

GRANIT: I don't know. I think I have already given my answer and as for my dear friend, Jack Eccles, he has from the beginning had a religious attitude. He has tried to harmonize it with science in his own way, and I think everyone should be allowed to think as he likes in these matters.

WHEELER: One comment and one question. I found it difficult in your fascinating talk to agree with one point—that we cannot think of a computer equaling the brain, and yet I would like to state why I nevertheless agree with your point. George Pugh has spelled out in detail all of the objections that have been raised in times past against the idea of making the equivalent of a brain in a computer. One by one he's knocked them down. But he left one out. Let's imagine we have it. What do we do with it? The child, the baby with its brain, is programmed by the mother, day after day, lovingly, learning how to walk, how to talk, how to clap its hands. Through long centuries of evolution, we've developed a cultural program in which the mother brings up the child. Now, if we come along with a computer with brainlike potential, what mother takes over its program? In other words, it's wrong to consider the computer or the brain in isolation. You have to consider it as part of the evolutionary community. And if it is bought into existence—bang!—and is no part of any evolutionary community—it's dead!

GRANIT: Yes, the mother operates in a process which is one of the greatest products of evolution, man's adaptability, which exceeds that of any other organism. Even monkeys don't have the adaptability we have, and I don't know how a computer could be adaptable in this way—if that plastic adaptability can be translated into logistics. It is such an essential function of our brain.

WHEELER: Could I ask my simple question? I looked at a book on the brain not so long ago. It gave the weight of the brain of an insect, it gave the weight of the brain of a dog, and the weight of the brain of man—an ascending scale, designed to make us proud of ourselves. However, when it came to the dolphin, it did not give the brain weight straight out. That would have diminished our pride. Instead, it spoke of the *ratio* of brain weight to body weight being less for the dolphin than for man. How is this?

GRANIT: The brain, of course, is not merely a weight, a thing that weighs something. It has specific areas. And that is why evolution has given us an advantage in giving us those areas where mentation takes place. I think it is wrong to take it as brain size merely. The Neanderthal man had a brain that was 100 cc bigger than our own. But much of it was in the wrong place, and perhaps the same thing is true for the dolphin.

AUDIENCE: Can man's will become strong enough to control his own evolution?

GRANIT: I think so. Not completely, of course, because there are other men's wills acting throughout society, and we must think of all these things in population terms. It's not one man developing, it's the population; but man's will may well introduce a remarkable prolification in the evolution.

RORTY: I think I am the only real friend the computers have on the platform. I would like to put in another word about what might be said for them. Consider the quotation from James which Professor Granit offered. James said the mind is just what one would expect from an organ which was added to control a nervous system grown too complex to control itself. One might, analogously, think of the program of the computer as just what was added to control hardware too complex to control itself. But that would be misleading, because that would suggest that the program was something besides the hardware. The program is just the way the thing is wired up, if you like to put it that way. It seems to me that what the advent of computers has done for reflection on the subject is to suggest, as Hilary Putnam did, that we think of the mind-body relation in terms of the program-hardware relation, rather than in terms of the relation between one organ and another organ.

If we think in those terms, I think we can follow Putnam in raising the following question: Suppose that we are visited by creatures from another planet, who explain to us that our species is itself a species which their species designed, built out of protoplasm, and programmed as self-reproducing automata in specifiable ways. They say to us: "You see, it is quite true, you have what you call consciousness, rational direction, will, and so forth. We built you that way. But what you don't have is this thing you call a mind, what you have is a program, i.e., the way we wired you up." Now, the view of mind, which I was saying yesterday is characteristic of this Ryle-Dennett tradition, suggests that you can drop the hypothesis of the creatures from another planet, and put in their place the ordinary evolutionary factors which brought our species into being (assuming that we do not have to postulate factors of another sort than Darwin knew about) and get roughly the same result! What we've got is not a mind but a program, that is, a way of being wired up. When one puts it in those terms, it comes to seem misleading to speak of the mind as a control organ which does what the too-complex hardware can't do. Because it *is* simply the complexity of the hardware. This is my brief little defense of computers. But in order to try to bring out the difference between this view and Professor Granit's, perhaps I could ask him a question. There seem to be two alternative ways of thinking of mind, or of the distinction between mind and body. One uses the analogy of a distinct organ brought in, as James puts it, to control what could not control itself. The other is the conception of the body as programmed, in the sense in which a computer is programmed. In this sense, the program can't be conceived of as a distinct organ. Do you adopt one of these views?

GRANIT: I see. Well, I think I take the former view. As I said, the logistic balance of the mind can be computerized to the last inch, if you are used to using these old measures. But the organizational origin must be considered original. I don't think that would be something that could be produced by a computer. Nor can we produce the adaptability by computer. And I think, in general, the effect of organization is something that alters things—when the molecules combine into an insulin structure, new properties appear. And in the same way, I think of mind appearing as a new property, and a kind of organization in nature which we cannot understand at this moment. This is my standpoint. If it isn't acceptable, is it clear to you what I mean?

RORTY: If I could press the argument one step further, it seems to me that both sides in the argument can agree that new properties emerge. That is, when you program a computer, it has properties which the unprogrammed hardware didn't have. But the question is, does it have something appropriately called the "extra organ", or does it have merely the need to be described in a new vocabulary in order to explain its activities—viz. a programmer's vocabulary as opposed to a hardware vocabulary?

GRANIT: Probably the latter.

WIGNER: I think new laws of nature will have to be introduced to describe the mind, and the present laws of nature do not describe it. That is the opinion of most physicists. [Wheeler shakes his head, no.] No? Well, that is my opinion. And, in my opinion, I know that new laws of nature will have to be introduced to describe the functioning of the mind. And I would not describe it as a new organ because a new organ is something separated from the rest, just as electricity is not something that has been introduced separately. It interacts with gravitation. It interacts with magnetism. It is then a duality, more complex, but better describing actual situations. It isn't something separate, just as electricity is not separate from the existence of other parts of physics, but is united with them, and plays a different role under different conditions. I think it is the same with the mind. Maybe I am wrong.

AUDIENCE: Is the mind more than the sum of its parts? Or have we not just realized the brain's continuing complexity in entirety?

GRANIT: I think the question very odd and useless in a way in the use of the word "sum." Sum has an imprecise meaning and doesn't tell us anything.

AUDIENCE: If the whole nerve brain complex operates on electricity, approximately 14 watts, is it possible that the brain has the capacity to broadcast and receive via wireless radio and that the human really does have the potential to communicate?

GRANIT: I am not an expert in extrasensory perception, and I do not think that that has been proved.

AUDIENCE: Is there a physiological model for the holographic theory of memory?

GRANIT: Well, you have to turn to Professor Pribram for that. He believes in that. I don't believe in that.

NOTES

1. W. Heisenberg, *Physik und Philosophie* (Frankfurt a/M: Verlag Ullsteim, 1973), p. 83.
2. W. James, *The Principles of Psychology*, Vol. 1 (New York: Macmillan, 1891), p. 144.
3. E. V. Evarts, *Journal of Neurophysiology* 29 (1966), pp. 1011–1027.
4. Charles Sherrington, *Man on His Nature*, The Gifford Lectures, Edinburgh, 1937–8 (New York: Macmillan; Cambridge, Eng.: Cambridge University Press, 1941).
5. Ernst Mayr, "The Emergence of Evolutionary Novelties," in *Evolution after Darwin*, ed. Sol Tax (Chicago: University of Chicago Press, 1960), Vol. 1, pp. 349–380, especially p. 374.
6. R. Granit, *The Purposive Brain* (Cambridge: MIT Press, 1977).
7. R. W. Doty, *Acta neurobiologiae experimentalis* 35 (1973), pp. 791–804.
8. W. Penfield, *Proceedings of the Association for Research in Nervous and Mental Disease*, 30 (1950), pp. 513–528.
9. Sherrington, *Man on His Nature*.
10. R. W. Sperry. The work published in *The Papal Acad. Sci.* 30 (1965) is more accessible in *In Brain and Conscious Experience*, ed. J. C. Eccles (Berlin: Springer-Verlag, 1966), pp. 298–313.
11. D. H. Ingvar and N. A. Lassen, *Brain Work* (Copenhagen: Munksgaard, 1975).
12. Ibid., pp. 397–413.
13. V. Mountcastle, *Johns Hopkins Medical Journal* 136 (1975), pp. 109–131.
14. H. Stephen, in *The Functional and Evolutionary Biology of Primates*, ed. R. Tuttle (Chicago: Aldine/Atherton, 1972), p. 162.
15. D. Ploog and T. Melnechuk, *Neurosciences Research Symposium Summaries* 6 (1970).
16. W. Penfield and T. Rasmussen, *The Cerebral Cortex of Man* (New York: Macmillan, 1950).
17. P. M. Daniel and D. Whitteridge, *Journal of Physiology* (London) 159 (1961), pp. 203–221.
18. S. M. Zeki, *Brain Research* 19 (1970), pp. 63-75.
19. H. A. Johnson, *Perspective in Biology and Medicine* 24 (1980), pp. 113–121.
20. Ingvar and Lassen, *Brain Work*.
21. A. Brodal, "The wiring patterns of the brain: Neuroanatomical experiences and their implications for general views of the organization of the brain," in *The Neurosciences: Paths of Discovery*, ed. F. G. Worden, J. P. Swazey, and G. Adelman (Cambridge: MIT Press, 1975).
22. James, *The Principles of Psychology*.
23. Sperry, *Brain and Conscious Experience*, pp. 298–313.
24. Granit, *The Purposive Brain*.
25. Rene Dubos, *Man Adapting*, Hepsa Ely Silliman Memorial Lectures, Yale University (New Haven: Yale University Press, 1965).

26. John C. Eccles, *The Human Psyche*, the Gifford Lectures (New York: Springer International, 1980).
27. E. Renan, *Dialogues et Fragments Philosophiques* (Paris: Calmann Levi, 1876), p. 97.

The Limitations of the Validity of Present-Day Physics

EUGENE WIGNER

Past Extensions of the Area of Physics

Let me begin by recalling how much the attitude toward, and the expectations from, science—and in particular physics—have changed in the three hundred years in which *our* physics was established. What I call "our physics" is its development in the last three hundred years, essentially since Newton's *Principia Mathematica Philosophiae Naturalis*.

This book formulated a few principles which are, if formulated mathematically, very simple. They led to a description of the motion of our sun's planets, and this description eventually proved to be accurate to about one part in 30,000, as far as the shapes of the planets' orbit are concerned. It is about equally accurate in other respects. Perhaps even more importantly, the same laws of nature which gave the properties of the planets' orbits also described the earth's attraction on the objects around us. Without any further assumption they described the laws of free fall—the laws first established by Galileo. There are, in addition, some small effects in the planets' orbits, entirely unexplained and largely also unobserved until Newton's time, which his laws permitted us to foresee. Altogether, Newton's gravitational theory was a marvelous success. And indeed, it attracted much attention and admiration.

Yet the limitations of the theory were not only recognized,

but were also taken for granted. The theory, for instance, did not describe electrical or magnetic phenomena, nor those of heat or the elastic and other properties of substances. But science was modest in those days, and a general principle which had at least two sets of valid and highly accurate consequences—in this case, planetary motion and free fall—was quite unexpected and deserved admiration.

I'll return to this observation later when I contrast our present high expectations from science with the much more modest ones of the earlier times. But before doing that, I'll give a description, though a very superficial one, of the changes our science, physics, underwent since its inception, since Newton's time. I'll do this because it is not unreasonable to expect that the character of future changes which may refer to the problem of the mind will have a similarity to the past ones. But even before doing this, let me tell you what I consider to be Newton's even greater accomplishment than that of the introduction of his law of gravitation. This is the sharp separation of initial conditions and laws of nature. The initial conditions describe the original state of a system, the laws of nature should describe only its development in time, i.e., its state at any later time, assuming the initial state is given. This separation of initial conditions and laws of nature is still with us; it is so much with us that we rarely emphasize the importance of this accomplishment of Newton—we take it for granted. The initial conditions are outside the area of physics and largely even of that of science—surely, it would not be reasonable to expect that a mathematically simple description of the color of the eyes of all the participants at this conference and the shapes of their noses, among many other things, can be derived from basic principles. But the sharp separability of laws of nature and initial conditions is surely not obvious, the discovery of the usefulness of this separation is a wonderful accomplishment of Newton—even if it should turn out at some future time that it is of approximate nature, as, according to Ernest Mach, all our recognitions are.

Let me now talk about the next extension of the area of physics, the scope of which I wish to indicate as well as the changes it introduced in physics' basic concepts. I am referring to Maxwell's equations which describe electric and magnetic phenomena, including the propagation of light, beautifully. Just as do Newton's ideas, these equations give a common basis to a number of experimental results. I may mention at least Ampere's and Faraday's laws.

But Maxwell's mathematical description of the possible states of a system was so different from Newton's that the straight unification of the two can hardly appear to lead to an attractive theory. Newton described the states, including the initial state and those appearing after a lapse of time, by the positions and velocities of the objects of the system considered, for instance those of the planets. Maxwell's equations describe the state by specifying the electric and magnetic field strengths at every point of space. Newton's equations' variables were numbers, six times as many as were objects present; Maxwell's equations refer to six functions of the three space coordinates, giving the three components of the electric and magnetic field strengths at every point of space. Further, Newton's equations accounted for the effects of gravitational forces, but disregarded electric and magnetic phenomena; Maxwell's equations carried the opposite restriction. It was realized already when Maxwell's equations were proposed that they might be usable together with those of Newton, but also that the two are not in harmony with each other. But separately, they were both very simple and elegant and their joint use was also very useful.

The next big progress that I wish to mention does not have the characteristic of the previous one. It was the introduction of statistical mechanics and therewith an explanation of the phenomenon of heat and of the laws of thermodynamics. The new assumptions that entered were those of the atomistic nature of matter and of laws of interaction between these atoms—mainly repulsion—very different from the gravitational one. But the description of the state of a system—

mainly of a gas—was that of Newtonian theory—the variables are the positions and velocities of the atoms. The success of statistical mechanics, principally kinetic theory of gases, was astounding (even though it was, at first, very unpopular), and it was an extension of the area of physics which was not based on a fundamentally new description of the state of a system but followed the older one, used already by Newton. Of course, there was some resistance against the introduction of atoms, and the denial of the continuous nature of matter; but the already available basic concepts of physics could be used in this case to extend the area of physics. This development is, therefore, an exception from the general rule that any extension of physics demands some basic idea and a new description of the objects to which it refers. But the objects to the behavior of which the theory was applied were considered to be queer and, if at all existing, not necessarily subject to the old and accepted theory.

It may be good to mention, though, that it was this theory, statistical mechanics, which gave an explanation of some properties of matter—in particular the specific heats and the connection between the viscosity and heat conductivity of gases. Until its introduction, but in many cases even much later, it was said that the properties of matter—those which I mentioned, but also chemical stability, density, strength, and all others—are not derivable from basic principles of physics: when their values are needed, they have to be looked up in suitable handbooks. I'll come back later to the fact of how much this has changed by another extension of the area of physics.

I will not discuss the next wonderful development, that of the introduction of the theory of relativity, because, wonderful as that was, it has not extended the area of physics. I come instead to the discussion of a development which took place largely during the period of my own efforts to contribute to physics' progress: the impact of quantum theory and, in particular, quantum mechanics on physics and also on science in general.

The extension of physics' area by the quantum mechanical theory was truly spectacular. As was mentioned before, for a long time the structure of matter, its properties, both the physical and even more the chemical, were considered to be outside of physics' area. I often mention a statement which was in the first physics book I read: "Atoms and molecules may exist, but they are outside the area of physics." Today, this sounds ridiculous. We have made successful efforts to derive the properties of atoms and molecules, in particular their spectra, from the equations of quantum mechanics—and the accuracy we achieved is spectacular. Their physical and chemical properties are now considered to be derivable from that theory, and many such derivations were successfully carried out. In fact, we believe that all physical and chemical properties, hence in fact all chemistry, are implicitly contained in the equations of quantum mechanics. They have not all been derived from its equations, because this would present too complex a mathematical problem; also because it would not be very interesting, for instance, to calculate the heat of vaporization of methyl ammonium sulfate. We believe that all this is intrinsically contained in our equations—just as the possible paths of meteorites are contained in Newton's equation. To have, fundamentally, encompassed all chemistry is a wonderful acheivement of physics.

Are the basic principles of quantum mechanics, including the description of the "state" of the systems considered, fundamentally different from those of the earlier theories? Indeed they are—the states are described either by vectors in an infinite dimensional so-called Hilbert-space, or, for simpler situations by "wave functions"—that is, complex functions in a space with three times more dimensions than are particles present in the system considered. This space is called "configuration space"—each of its points corresponds to a possible configuration of the particles of a system, but in virtually all actual states a continuous manifold of all configurations is present. Another fundamental change is that even though some definite states, that is, states with some definite wave functions, can be experimentally produced, if a system in an arbitrary state is given, there is no way to ascertain its wave function, i.e., its state. This is a truly basic departure from all earlier theories and, in fact, all measurements carried out on a system will change its quantum mechanical state, i.e. its wave function or state vector. And, as perhaps J. C. Bell has shown most convincingly, the quantum mechanical description of states cannot be replaced by a primitive one.

Well, I finish herewith the description of the past extensions of the area of physics. I hope I have presented convincing evidence that most of these extensions altered the principles of the earlier theories basically. The last extension I mentioned—quantum mechanics—constitutes a radical departure from classical concepts. Now, even though this is not truly our subject, I will say a few words about the wonderful nature of our ability to develop these theories, but also about their weaknesses and lack of consistency.

The Existence of Science: A Miracle in Spite of Lack of Perfection

As was mentioned before, "our science" is only about three hundred years old and, perhaps, I add that science in general is probably only a few thousand years old—surely this does apply to the traditional Greek geometry. Man is several hundred thousand years old—what was it that induced him, quite suddenly, to develop science? We do not know—it is a puzzle, as most instability phenomena are. Surely, our science was not necessary to assure man's survival in the Darwinian sense. No other animal has developed a science even vaguely similar to ours—it is not needed for survival.

It is clear that science has changed the lifestyle of man drastically. Did it increase his happiness? Einstein said: no. But the acquisition of science, and the contributions to it, surely did. Does it create some danger to the existence of man? We surely hope not, but we should probably watch it—it does have some dangerous ingredients.

The development of science, in particular physics, is miraculous for another reason: every step in its development shows that the preceding theory was valid only approximately, and valid approximately only under certain conditions. Newton's theory is valid with a high accuracy if only gravitational forces play a role, all pre-quantum theories are valid only for macroscopic bodies and for these only under certain conditions. It is lucky that such special conditions exist under which simplified approximate theories present a wonderfully good approximation. Surely, if macroscopic theories had not been developed, it would have been even more difficult, perhaps impossible, to develop quantum mechanics. General relativity would not have been invented, not even by Einstein, had the original theory of gravitation not existed.

How close are our present theories to perfection? Surely, they are wonderful, and even their contribution to overcome the physical problems of life, to provide food and shelter for every man, is remarkable. But are they, is in particular our physics, even self-consistent? The answer to this question is rarely publicized, but it surely is: no. The general theory of relativity is based on the assumption of the meaningfulness of the space-time point concept defined by the crossing of two world-lines, yet it is easy to show that quantum mechanics does not permit the definition of such points. The basic idea of the fundamental interpretation of quantum mechanics postulates the process of "measurement." Yet it is easy to show that the existence of this process is not consistent with the principles of quantum mechanics. We'll return to this point.

Are these facts—and some others—surprising or alarming? To me, they are surely surprising when I first realized them. But, actually, it was a wonderful gift to be provided with situations in which the laws of nature in very simplified form were excellent approximations. Without being provided with such situations, physics, in particular, could not have been developed by man. Is it alarming to realize that all laws of nature we know, and also those we will know, are, quite surely, only approximately valid? I believe not. In fact, if science were completed, the satisfaction which research, the furthering of human knowledge, had provided, would disappear. Also, even more men would strive for power and domination. It is good that the completion of our scientific knowledge is an unattainable ideal. Striving toward it is attracting many of us, and gives us much pleasure and satisfaction. I wish this were much more generally recognized.

Let me now return to our real subject—the place of mind in nature, which also constitutes the most important limitation of present-day physics.

A Concept Outside the Area of Present-Day Physics: The Mind

In order to be completely honest, let me admit first that present-day physics is not perfect even in its acknowledged areas. Quantum mechanics is not in complete harmony with the theories of relativity, particularly not the general one. And even quantum mechanics alone still lacks the complete simplicity which we are striving for—in spite of the accomplishments of the past, particularly those of Salam and Weinberg, we still have several types of interactions, not united into a single equation, and there are other grave problems. But this is not the question on which I wish to report to you now: that problem concerns an area to which physics has not yet been extended.

As was mentioned before, there is no way to bring a system with absolute certainty into a definite prescribed quantum state, nor is there any process by which its quantum state can be determined if it is, to begin with, an arbitrary one. How can we then verify quantum theory in detail? The answer is: by a succession of measurements, also called observations. A very typical such measurement or observation is the so-called Stern-Gerlach experiment, which tells the observer whether the spin of the atom on which the measurement is carried out is parallel or antiparallel to the magnetic field of the measuring apparatus. If the spin turns out, let us say, to be parallel to that magnetic field, and is then remeasured with a second Stern-Gerlach apparatus, the magnetic field of which is parallel to that of the first one, the answer will be again "parallel." But if the magnetic field of the second apparatus is in any other direction, the answer cannot be foreseen with certainty—quantum mechanics only gives the probabilities for the two possible outcomes of the second measurement. The same would be true with respect to a third measurement.

This is a description of the probabilistic outcome of the simplest quantum mechanical measurement. However, the situation is the same with respect to all such measurements except that, as a rule, many more than two outcomes are possible. Since the quantum mechanical equation describing the time-development of a system is deterministic, this appears to be—and is—a contradiction. It could be resolved by the assumption that the initial state of the measuring apparatus is uncertain, which it may well be. But this does not help: it follows from the linear nature of the present quantum mechanical equation for time development that if the apparatus is in a state in which it gives the correct result, and if the object is in a state in which the outcome is determined (as it was in the Stern-Gerlach case for the second apparatus with a magnetic field parallel to that of the first one), the interaction thereof with the object in a different state does not give a definite result. It only establishes a correlation between the state of the apparatus and that of the object so that a measurement of the former's and of the latter's states—if such a measurement can be carried out—would give consistent results. But just after the original measurement, neither the appartus nor the object are in definite states but in "superpositions" of such.

This is indeed the case and has been verified for some very simple measurements with very small apparata. But surely a living person can not be in such a superposition—if I look at a screen I see a flash either on the left or on the right side—I am never in a superposition of having seen it on the two sides.

This shows, certainly, that quantum mechanics does not describe my impressions and I assume that it does not describe those of any truly living person either. It is quite possible that quantum mechanics' domain of validity is even further limited—the Russian physicist V. Fock said that the measuring apparata must be described classically, i.e. that quantum mechanics, and hence present-day physics, does not describe measuring apparata correctly. I may return to this question later.

This sharply contradicts the theory of "dialectical materialismus," which postulated the validity of an even earlier, and hence even less encompassing, physics to the phenomenon of life. That was a very demanding postulation, quite in contrast with the early and very modest evaluation of science which was mentioned in connection with Newton's work. That a completion of science, as the dialectical materialismus assumed, would not be even desirable from a human point of view, was also mentioned before.

What are then the limitations of the validity of present-day physics as far as life and consciousness and "mind" are concerned? It is possible to assume that physics loses validity completely if the phenomenon of life plays a role. But this is in conflict with the work of our wonderful biologists who have described the life and multiplication at least of one-celled creatures quite well. And past experience with the extension of the area of physics tells us that the validity of our theories has no sharp boundary. I believe therefore that present-day physics and chemistry may well be very useful to describe very primitive modes of life, but it loses validity increasingly as we go to more developed animals with active minds and consciousnesses. Such a transition exists also in stars on the surface of which only gravitational forces play a significant role, whereas the electromagnetic forces and light pressure and also nuclear forces become dominant as we go further and further inside. Of course, the validity of approximate theories decreases also as we extend the time-period of their application.

The question naturally arises whether it is only life that

limits the validity of physics and, in particular, of quantum mechanics. I will admit that I thought so until reading an article by D. Zeh which calls attention to the fact that the quantum mechanical description (i.e., the wave function or state vector) of macroscopic bodies is greatly influenced, that is, altered, even by microscopic objects, in fact by atoms, rather far away. This means that, in our world in which there is about one hydrogen atom in every cubic yard even in intergalactic space, macroscopic systems cannot be "isolated," their states are subject to outside and largely uncontrollable influences. Since present-day physics applies only to isolated systems, we may have here an even narrower limit to the validity of our science, it may be that determinism is not truly valid for macroscopic systems beyond rather short time intervals. My own calculation shows that a cubic centimeter solid's wave function is grossly altered by the cosmic radiation in a small fraction of a second even in intergalactic space. Of course, we are never interested in the wave function of a macroscopic body, but it seems worthwhile to realize this—a limitation of present-day physics' validity which suggests an indeterministic theory. In fact, I have proposed an equation therefore. But I must admit that this equation also completely fails to describe the phenomena of life, such as pain and pleasure, sorrow and enjoyment.

Another problem I wish to mention in connection with our very general subject is that of a possible limitation of the human mind and intelligence. We know that there are facts and insights which we cannot communicate to animals—no animal is familiar, for instance, with the associative law of multiplication. Since, according to Darwin, we are also animals, is it not possible that our understanding of nature also has limitations? Let me say that I hope that, even if this should be true, we will be able to continue the extension of our knowledge indefinitely, we will be able to do so even if the limit thereof will always remain widely separated from the complete knowledge and understanding of Nature. After all, it is entirely possible that beyond our realization of as yet unexplained phenomena, such as that of the mind and consciousness, there is a wealth of other phenomena which we suspect as little as we did the evidence for the existence of quarks twenty-five years ago. But, in spite of all this, I continue to hope that knowledge, both the acquisition and the creation thereof, will continue to give pleasure to man.

Let me finish by telling you in this connection that I very much support the institution of a certain type of science club. I participated in such a club as a high school student in Hungary and many others were started in Italy, actually by someone I do not admire: Benito Mussolini. These clubs had a meeting every week, or every other week, and someone delivered an address on a subject essentially of his own choice. I spoke, at our high school club, on the theory of relativity. The speeches were followed by a discussion and if there was no discussion it was clear that the speaker did not convey the ideas he spoke of to the members of the club. But there was a discussion after almost every presentation and it gave pleasure to the listeners and some satisfaction to the speaker. In this way the acquisition and the imparting of knowledge had a very satisfactory effect. I wish and hope that such get-togethers will be widely revived.

WIGNER: *Conversations*

ELVEE: I will take the liberty of beginning this conversation. I came to this conference a new believer in the religion of quantum mechanics and you have introduced certain doubts this last hour. Are you telling me that quantum mechanics does not apply to Schrödinger's cat?

WIGNER: Yes, I think it does not apply to Schrödinger's cat. In my opinion, life is a phenomenon similar to other phenomena which may be present very superficially and in very small amounts as it is in bacteria and viruses. But in developed organisms it plays a decisive role. Just as nuclear phenomena have little effect on the surfaces of stars, so as we go on to more complicated animals, it applies less and less and describes less and less. Would you refute this?

ELVEE: John Wheeler. Help!

WHEELER: Well, I enjoy Eugene Wigner's approach so much that I would not like to attack; I wish him well. I don't think it will work, the idea that life is something magic outside of physics.

WIGNER: No, only outside of present-day physics! Just as electricity and magnetism were outside of Newton's physics. Just as microscopic phenomena were outside of the physics which I first learned, I think life is outside of present-day physics. You don't agree with this?

WHEELER: I think it would be useful to compare the attitude of my wonderful colleague Eugene Wigner on quantum mechanics with that of Niels Bohr. I will illustrate by reference to the road map we used to get from Minneapolis to St. Peter and this Lund Arena. Professor Wigner, as you may know, is not only a member of the Princeton Mathematics Department, but also the Physics Department. So if you give him this map and you drive the car, he will object when he gets here because the map doesn't show him how to get the car into the auditorium. In quantum mechanics, the mathematical formalism of quantum theory, he objects, does not get him to the end of the story about making a quantum mechanical measurement. The rest of us get out of the car outside and walk in. Niels Bohr gets out of the car of the equations of quantum mechanics, outside the measurement process and says, "Look, this is the way it is, it has to be an act of magnification, an irreversible act of amplification, before we can measure." This is not an objection to your point of view, Eugene, it is a description of differences.

WIGNER: I don't know, it seems to me that the fact that quantum mechanics is so far removed from the phenomena of life and that it has no operator for pain or pleasure or for anything else, is already "outside." There is a mathematical proof that as long as quantum mechanics is valid, no measurement has a definite result. But measurements do have a definite result. So, apparently there is some trouble with quantum mechanics. And it would not be good if we had a complete science because then what should Professor Wheeler discover next? He couldn't discover anything.

WHEELER: I think it would help everybody a little bit to make a distinction between mathematics of quantum theory and the practical use of quantum theory.

WIGNER: Yes, the practical use of quantum theory does not cause the problem, because we don't assume that it is valid under all conditions. But where is the dividing line between prediction and measurement? You know that for the phenomenon that we observe, that of the pointer position for instance, we obtain a definite result. This is what Von Neumann called the collapse of the wave function. And it does collapse. But where it collapses, whether it collapses when we observe its position, or whether it collapses even before the pointer approaches the point of its final position, we don't know. And this is the difficulty, and this is the problem.

WHEELER: Where you get out of the car and walk in, that's the problem.

AUDIENCE QUESTION: If life is outside of present-day physics, at what point do the principles of present-day physics fail, and allow the mind to exert its influence in determining its own existence?

WIGNER: No form of life is described by present-day physics. Similarly, Newton's theory did not describe light. Just the same, the information about the positions of the planets came to us through light, and the fact that something is not incorporated into present-day physics does not mean that we should not deal with it and we should not accept its consequences. Similarly, even though a context may hold, my wave function collapses, or how it is that I *do* see the flash either above or below, and am *not* in a super position. I can't explain that, but I accept the result of it. And, if it flashed above, I am sure the spin is directed above, and if it flashes below, I am sure the spin is directed downward. In other words, the fact that some phenomenon is not yet incorporated into the basic principles of physics does not mean that we should close our eyes to it.

AUDIENCE: Do you think that quantum mechanics may be superseded someday by a theory that is more deterministic?

WIGNER: Can I be honest? If I am honest, I do not believe it, because what I learn from Dieter Zeh is that there is a universal interaction and, therefore, determinism is not positivistical or supportable. We can't find a wave function for the universe. There are no macroscopic isolated systems. Therefore, the isolation of initial conditions from the laws of nature, which I consider the greatest accomplishment of Newton, will not remain indefinitely valid. It will turn out to be an approximation. Everything we learn is an approximation.

AUDIENCE: If you say that the indeterminacy of elementary particles is irrelevant to the human mind when the mind is identified with the mass of the brain, is it possible to conceive of the mind as a novel individual, arising from brain activity, but still interacting causally with the brain? Then, could not the quantum theory apply to human minds or perhaps to human freedom?

WIGNER: Well, how quantum mechanics will be changed and extended, I don't know. Perhaps it will be called quantum mechanics if what you suggest is so, but at present, quantum mechanics surely does not explain the human mind and the human brain. It is possible to believe that the motion of atoms in our brain is reasonably well explained by quantum mechanics, but I don't think so. I think the fact of mind has even a physical effect, just as electricity and magnetism have an effect on bodies which are mostly governed by gravitational forces. Similarly, I think the effect of the mind also makes the present laws of physics invalid under conditions in which thinking, feeling, pains, and pleasure play a role. I don't know whether anybody agrees with me, but I believe it is this way. I know that Professor Wheeler probably does not. Right? Professor Wheeler does not.

AUDIENCE: Returning to a statement in your lecture, why don't you believe that relativity changed the nature of science?

WIGNER: No, I didn't try to say that. I said that it did not extend the area of science. In other words, Maxwell's theory and its predecessors extended science to electric and magnetic phenomena and to the propagation of light. Quantum mechanics extended it, among other things, to chemistry. Relativity theory changed some basic concepts wonderfully and beautifully, but it did not extend the area of science.

AUDIENCE: Does the present-day physicist in Hungary have the academic and scientific freedom to pursue this theoretical approach you have?

WIGNER: I think so, I think so. I was there and I spoke with them, and they reacted quite normally and told me what they object to and so on, but I am afraid on the whole that they agreed with me. I mentioned in my manuscript that the conceit of science has increased tremendously. In Newton's times it was naturally taken for granted that it is limited, but dialectical materialism tried to claim that it has explained everything. And I am afraid I disagree with that very strongly. It would not be good if we knew everything.

AUDIENCE: Is time the boundary we must escape in order to see how quantum theory applies to modern physics on the macro level?

WIGNER: This is not in my discussion, but I think that space-time or even space alone imagined as infinitely dividable is not valid in physics. I think eventually we will quantize space also, and we won't have an infinite subdivision of space. I believe that part of the difficulties of quantum field theories, the need for renormalization, is evidence that some change, some fundamental change of this nature, will have to be introduced. I tried to work on it, but I must frankly tell you that I was not successful.

Spirit and Mind

WOLFHART PANNENBERG

The notion of spirit and reflections on the spiritual nature of the mind do not enjoy a place of particular prominence in the modern philosophical discussion of the concept of mind. This may be due to a deliberate avoidance of unwanted connotations reminding of certain traditional beliefs in spiritual substances beside and behind the material world. It is the conjecture of this paper, however, that a discussion of the difference and connections between mind and spirit may be helpful in exploring and clarifying the relationship between mind and body, which in recent years has become more of an open question again than many would have assumed some decades ago. Besides, a discussion of the difference and connection between mind and spirit enables theology to enter into the picture and dispute over mind and body and to contribute to the question concerning the place of mind in nature.

The obvious context of the mind-body problem in the history of modern thought is, of course, the Cartesian doctrine of two substances, *res cogitans* and *res extensa*. Karl Popper has shown that, on the basis of Descartes's theory of matter and of the mechanical movements of bodies, it became inexplicable how the immaterial soul could conceivably move the body.[1] And he pointed out further how this difficulty gave rise to the various theories of a parallelism of mind and body, from the Occasionalists through Spinoza to Leibniz. The Cartesian dualism also became the occasion of the attempts of

physicalism as proving the assumption of a second substance, mind, to be superfluous. In philosophy, this tendency was greatly promoted by David Hume's criticism of
the conception of mind as a substance. While in the early
days of British empiricism John Locke believed the notion of
mind as a special, spiritual substance to arise from the operations we experience in ourselves, just as evidently as the
notion of body arises from "those simple ideas we have from
without,"[2] Hume considered the notion of mind as a particular substance to be "absolutely unintelligible," since he as-
sured us that we have no impression of a mind comparable to
the sense impressions that lead to perceptions of external
objects.[3] Under the impact of physicalism and behaviorism
the pressures towards a reduction of the notion of mind to
functions and epiphenomena of bodily processes increased,
and in recent decades philosophical language analysis contributed a further argument to the same result by reducing
the self to a mode of speech, the "index word" I. Thus Gilbert
Ryle, in his famous book on the concept of mind, could scoff
at "the myth of the ghost in the machine." Hence, there was a
great deal of surprise when Karl Popper confessed to his
belief in the ghost in the machine and, together with John
Eccles, reformulated a dualist and interactionalist model of
the relation between mind and body, especially between
mind and brain on the basis of Eccles's neurological description of the human brain. The book they published together
on *The Self and Its Brain* reopened the discussion of the issue.[4]

Popper's main argument against physicalism or materialism
is that, at least in the more radical forms of that interpretation
of nature, not only the reality of consciousness is denied, but
especially the existence of technological artifacts and other
objects of human culture cannot be accounted for in such a
way as to do justice to their specifically logical structure and
form of construction. Nor is physicalistic behaviorism able to
account for the higher functions of language, i.e., for its
descriptive and argumentative functions.[5]

The positive complement of this critique of physicalism is

the interpretation of the evolution of life and even of cosmic evolution in terms of a process of *emergence*,[6] where random events sometimes bring about a new epoch under the selective pressures of the environment. Emergent qualities, therefore, are something new and unpredictable. Following Sir Alister Hardy's organic theory of evolution, Popper believes that in this way changes in behavior can also become selective factors in the evolutionary process.[7] This provides the general basis for his more specific thesis that linguistic behavior became a selective factor in the evolution of the human race: "the evolution of language can be explained, it seems, only if we assume that even a primitive language can be helpful in the struggle for life," and "language, once created, exerted the selection pressure under which emerged the human brain and the consciousness of self."[8]

The emergence of self-consciousness, then, and of the self-conscious mind, is based on language rather than the other way round. This also applies to the development of the individual person: "We are not born as selves; but . . . we have to learn to be selves."[9] That is not only a matter of language. The acquisition of language presupposes the discovery of the world through perception and especially the development of a sense for the constancy of objects, of spacial relations, and for identity in time. But the culmination of all this is the learning of a language. Thus: "Temporally, the body is there before the mind. The mind is a later achievement. . . ."[10]

This view of the emergence of the self-conscious mind from language, and therefore from a socio-cultural environment, reminds strongly of the thought of G. H. Mead, who also considered the self as arising from social interaction and especially from language. But Popper is more radical than Mead was. According to Popper's argument, it is not only some conception of ourselves, but the human mind as such that arises from the social world and especially through the acquisition of language, although of course there are hereditary predispositions for such a process.

To me, this conjectural account for the emergence of self-consciousness seems highly suggestive. There are, of course, problems. One of these problems is that it becomes necessary to distinguish strictly between consciousness and self-consciousness, since language certainly presupposes sense perception. And, indeed, in his dialogues with John Eccles, Popper repeatedly stressed that distinction between consciousness and self-consciousness, and he indicated at the same time that it is only self-consciousness that is to be considered a human privilege, while momentary consciousness in connection with perceptional activity should be attributed also to the higher animals.[11] The notion of mind, then, as emerging first from language, is to be strictly and intimately related to self-consciousness in distinction from consciousness in general.

Another problem appears in some places where Popper characterizes the world of culture and language—World 3, as he calls it, in terms of the world of the contents of thought and of "the products of the human mind."[12] What is the status of language in this context? If the human mind arises first through language, then it is certainly conceivable that some feedback of the human mind on the development and use of language may occur, but language as such cannot simply be described any longer as a product of the mind. Otherwise, the emergence of mind would be explained by a factor which itself takes its origin from mind. If the human mind first emerges through language, then in the origin of language there must be something prior to mind, but nevertheless also different from physical reality, since the distinction of the mind from physical reality is derived from it. The field, wherein the formation of language occurs, may be called a spiritual field. This does not seem inappropriate, because the terms "spiritual" and "spirit" should not be restricted to the religious life. There is a long-standing usage of the term spirit in relation to intellectual activities. But the religious dimension is also important. In the origins of human culture as well as in the development of the individual, the formulation of lan-

guage seems closely related to the origins of religious awareness. If this is the field from where the mind emerges, it may
be appropriately called a field of spiritual awareness.

The meaning of the word spirit has become vague and
opaque in our secular culture. Its potential has to be recovered
first, before it can be used. Therefore, it is necessary to make
explicit at least a few aspects of the spectrum of thought
which is connected with the word "spirit" and may be present in its connotations.

In the history of western philosophy, the notion of spirit
has been often restricted more or less to the concept of mind.
Thus, according to Locke, "The ideas we have belonging and
peculiar to spirit, are thinking and will, or a power of putting
body into motion by thought and, which is consequent to it,
liberty." It is by "putting together the ideas of thinking and
willing" that "we have the idea of an immaterial spirit,"[13] and
therefore Locke attributed the "operations of the mind" to a
"substance," which he called "spirit."[14] But as early as in
Augustine, the term "spirit" was used as an equivalent to
mind (*mens*),[15] and according to Thomas Aquinas, the
human soul is called spiritual or spirit because of her intellectual potential.[16] However, Thomas Aquinas was still
aware of a broader concept of spirit, which has an application
even to material things and processes: It expresses the intuition of impulse and motion.[17] It was a late echo of this
broader concept of spirit, when in the eighteenth and early
nineteenth centuries, spirit was taken as the animating principle of life,[18] before in Hegel's thought the power of spirit
was bound up with the dynamics of concept and idea and the
post-Hegelians reduced it again to the individual mind.

The most important source of that broader concept of spirit
was undoubtedly the Bible, where spirit—the spirit of God—
is conceived in analogy to the dynamics of the wind (John 3:8;
cf. Gen. 1:2; Ez. 37:9 f) and is understood as the principle of
life: According to Psalm 104, it is the spirit of God who
reneweth the surface of the ground in springtime, and all
creatures die, when God takes away the share of the spirit

given to them (29 f). In a simliar way, according to the older story of the creation of man, God breathes the "breath of life" into his nostrils (Gen. 2:7). It is only this breath of life which makes the human body a "living being" or, more literally, a "living soul" (Gen. 2:7). Elsewhere, this breath of life is identified as the divine spirit *(ruah)*, which is given by God and returned to him when the human person dies (Eccl. 12:7), just as the Gospel of Luke reports that Jesus died with the words of Ps. 31:6: "Father, into thy hands I commend my spirit" (Luke 23:46). The conception of the divine spirit as origin of life comes to powerful expression in the prophet Ezekiel's vision of the resurrection of the dead, strongly reminiscent of the origin of human life according to the Genesis story: "The dry bones of the people of Israel come alive when the wind or spirit from God breathes into them" (Ez. 37:5 f and 10, cf. 14). [19] And it is in the line of these ideas that the famous words of the Apostle Paul are to be understood that, while the first Adam was created a living being (according to Genesis 2:7), the last Adam became lifegiving spirit: "Therefore the body of the risen Lord and of those who will be raised with him is a spiritual body" (1 Cor. 15:45). In the context of the Old Testament thought about spirit and life, the notion of a spiritual body can only mean that there will be a form of life which is no longer separate from the divine spirit, the origin of life, but remains in unity with that origin. Therefore, Paul expects the new life of the resurrection to be immortal (1 Cor. 15:53 ff). In distinction from this hope for life in unity with God, the present life is not immortal, because it does not stay in unity with God, although it also owes its origin to God's life-giving spirit. This is Paul's idea of a "living being" in the present order of reality: It originates from the divine spirit, the giver of all life, but it is a separate reality departing from that origin and therefore mortal. It is within this framework that one has to interpret other distinctions of the Apostle between the human and the divine, between human spirit or mind *(nous)* and the spirit of God (1 Cor. 2:11 f, cf. 1 cor. 14:14 f).

The Pauline reinterpretation of the place of the divine Spirit in biblical anthropology became an important subject in early patristic thought. The discussions of the Christian fathers took place in an intellectual climate, where the Stoic concept of a divine pneuma, pervading the cosmos and manifest in the logical nature of the human soul, came close to the biblical ideas of the life-giving spirit of God, and the later Platonic idea of the divine character of the *Nous* or mind converged to a certain degree with the Genesis account of the creation of the human soul by the breath of God's spirit. The gnostics combined the Genesis account and Platonism to the effect that they considered the human soul of the chosen ones as participating in the divine nature of the *pneuma* from the moment of creation. The church fathers, on the other hand, considered participation in the divine *pneuma* as a matter of salvation rather than of creation. The natural human person, even his or her mind, has no share in the divine spirit. Nevertheless, the fathers had to admit that the created mind is related to and its life is constituted by the creative presence of God's spirit. The human mind is in need of being illumined by the divine spirit, and its disposition for the spirit is fully actualized only through salvation, through the pouring out of God's spirit into the hearts of the faithful, be it in the act of baptism—as Clement of Alexandria thought —or in the process of sanctification which only starts with baptism, according to the teaching of Origen.[20] But even in those in whom the divine spirit takes permanent dwelling, the spirit does not become part of their nature, but moves and activates them by his divine power.[21]

According to Christian patristics, then, there always remains a difference between the mind—which is sometimes called the human spirit—and the divine spirit. This is a somewhat restrictive interpretation of the biblical words that speak of a share of the human soul in the Spirit of God. It is a limited share, of course, because human life, like all living creatures, is under the power of death. This limitation was emphasized by Paul in contrast to the life to come, which will be permanently united to the life-giving spirit. Patristic theology also was anxious to emphasize the limitations of the natural man's share in the spirit, because the church fathers considered the endowment with the spirit's presence an achievement peculiar to salvation. But they admitted that a special kinship exists, indeed, between the human soul and God's spirit, and they went beyond the Pauline statements in attributing that kinship specifically to the mind. Thus, the mind not only originates from God's spirit like all living beings do, but it is also disposed to receive the illumination of the spirit in different stages up to the permanent indwelling of the spirit in the human soul.

All this, of course, is history. Does it have any significance for the interpretation of contemporary experience? Can the distinctive and dynamic interrelation of mind and spirit serve as a model, as a source of inspiration, when it comes to the contemporary problems of understanding the function of mind, its origin, and its relation to the human body and brain? In such a way the theologian should use biblical materials and conceptualities as well as the Christian teaching of the past: They should be treated not as dogmatic definitions, but as a source of inspiration for an appropriate understanding of present experience. Certain models derived from this tradition may be refuted by present experience. Still, the theologian will continue to look to the Bible and to the teaching of the church in confidence that from the wealth of that tradition, further clues for more adequate solutions of the problems may be obtained.

One possible advantage of interpreting the dependence of mind on the cultural process in general and on language in particular in terms of a spiritual origin of mind was mentioned before we set out to recover from history the latent potential of the notion of spirit in relation to the human soul: Such an interpretation could help to avoid a vicious circle in explaining the origin of mind by reference to culture and language, while culture and language in their turn are commonly understood to be products of the mind. But now, after some clarifications of the concept of spirit have been obtained, it becomes doubtful whether its meaning really applies to the problem of mind and language, of mind and culture. First of all, the biblical notion of spirit is related to the understanding of life and to the question of its origin, not primarily to human culture. However, certain extraordinary cultural achievements, especially the work of the artist, are said to require an extraordinary endowment with the divine spirit (Exod. 28:3; 31:3; 35:31), just as the achievement of heroes and the responsibilities of social leaders, especially of the king. Further, in this category belongs the charisma of the prophet, of the poet, and of the wise man. The vision of the prophet, as well as his words, comes from divine inspiration. But do these extraordinary phenomena admit the generalized assertion that all cultural phenomena and especially language in general indicate the presence and activity of the divine spirit in the human person? It seems that the statement in the older creation story about the endowment of Adam with the divine spirit does indeed present us with such a generalization. It is true, the story speaks of the breath of life. But on the other hand, it is the distinction of the human person from other creatures that is expressed that way. The creation story does not explicitly relate the divine endowment of Adam with the breath of life to the phenomenon of language, which is mentioned only later, when the story tells that God brought the animals he created to Adam in order "to see what he would call them; and whatever the man called every living creature, that was its name" (Gen. 2:19). Language is described here as an invention of man, as Johann Gottfried von Herder insisted, rather than as a supernatural gift of God, but one must not forget that the constitution of the human soul by the divine breath of life stands at the beginning of this story. Human invention and divine inspiration are not mutually exclusive, but divine inspiration activates the spiritual power of the human mind.

In the contemporary discussion, the relation between language and religion is rarely given the attention the phenomenon deserves. The dialogues between John Eccles and Karl Popper on mind and its origin are no exception in this respect. They mention a few times the myth-making activity of the human mind alongside other cultural activities, but they do not assign a special function to it comparable, say, to Ernst Cassirer's theory of symbolic forms. Cassirer saw myth at the origins of language, although language as we know it is no longer a magical incantation of reality. That mystical origin of language seems to be of special importance for the descriptive function of human language, which Popper stresses as the distinctively human element in language: The naming of an object is originally an ecstatic event, because in its name the object itself is thought to be present.[22] This hypothesis of Cassirer's has been corroborated by certain findings of J. Piaget in his research on the acquisition of language in the intellectual development of children. Piaget found that the early development of language is intimately related to play where the real object is represented symbolically by the toy, and he also found "mythical" and "animistic" elements in the intuitive thinking and talking of children until their seventh year.[23] Moreover, Piaget emphasizes the function of these phenomena in the acquisition of an awareness of an objective world, within which the child's own body and person take their place. All this is the more remarkable in view of the fact that Piaget does not only not refer to Cassirer in this connection, but has no intention to develop anything like a theory of a religious origin of language. He need not think of such an explanation, because he is accustomed to talk as if the child were a subject in its own right almost from the day of birth. This would presuppose that the human mind is already there from birth so that all experiences could be explained as actions of that subject. But if the human mind is no substance or primordial subject of our experiences, but emerges only in the course of our discovery of the world around us, especially of the social and cultural world, as Karl Popper suggests, so that the mind is comparable to the phenomenon of a flame that nourishes itself from the combustible material within its reach, then the origin of the self-conscious mind itself has to be looked for in the early acquisition of that world, and then, as far as language is concerned, the mythical and religious spirituality in the process of acquiring language becomes important. Such a spirituality may have surrounded also the first origins of language in the history of the human race.[24] Certain peculiarities of language, especially in its descriptive function, are better explained in such a perspective than on the assumption that language was formed in the service of toolmaking or hunting.[25]

The biblical concept of the divine spirit as origin of mind seems particularly interesting in relation to another problem connected with the descriptive function of language: How does one explain the fact that human mind and language are fit to grasp the reality of things as they really are? The possibility of truth in human statements would cause no great problem, if the human mind were completely passive and receptive in its perceptions. But today we know that, on the contrary, the mind and the brain are active in every moment of experience, starting with sense-perception. How is it possible that nevertheless the information we receive from the outside is not hopelessly distorted? On the basis of the biblical conception of spirit and mind, the answer could be that the same spirit that the human mind shares is also the origin of "life" in the beings outside ourselves, the creative origin of their particular "Gestalt." Something like this may underly the enigmatic remark in the creation story that "whatever the man called every living creature, that was its name" (Gen. 2:19). If we recall that to the archaic mind the name of a thing comprises its nature, this biblical phrase means nothing less but that the human person, on the basis of his or her participation in the divine spirit, is able to grasp the nature of things. Here it becomes important that the concept of spirit functions not only as origin of mind. Precisely because the spirit is the source of life at large, it can become the origin of mind, too, that grasps the reality of all "living beings."

The range of the mind's perceptive power extends beyond

the living beings to everything real, although it may have a special affinity to the nature of organisms, since the human mind is itself a "living soul" (Gen. 2:7). The explanation of the intelligibility of inorganic things may be analogous: They also took their origin from the creator spirit, although they are not animated by that spirit intrinsically as is true of the living beings. This throws a peculiar light on contemporary statements to the effect that modern physics does no longer offer a materialistic description of the universe. In commenting on the transition of physics from the concept of body to the field concept and to its attempts at explaining matter itself, Karl Popper says: "Materialism transcends itself."[26] On the basis of similar arguments, the German physicist Georg Sübmann says: "the material of all things appears like a web out of thought."[27] This is not an idealistic statement. Rather, the spiritual dynamics in the natural processes make it possible to understand how the human mind is able to grasp their structure and to make himself master of them.

Sübmann accepts that there is a correlation between spirit and life, if only one allows for a sufficiently broad concept of life. He distinguishes degrees of interiorization of the spiritual dynamics, starting not with plants and animals, but already before with physical streams and currents and continuing with the vegetative and sensitive life of plants and animals, before with the human spirit it comes to intellectual life.[28] But what can be taken as characteristic of a living entity as well as of the human mind, so that the capability of the mind to grasp the nature of things would be better understood?

One such characteristic seems to be bound up with the notion of *wholeness* or *Gestalt*. Each living being is a *Gestalt*, but it also perceives other things in terms of its form. There are primitive forms of Gestalt perception, dependent on just a few abstract characters. They may be related to hereditary schemes of perception, and the occurrence of such perceptions may evoke equally hereditary responses. But particular Gestalt perceptions may also be acquired by processes of learning, and the act of perception may go together with some more or less tacit awareness of the elements that are essential to that particular Gestalt. Most forms of Gestalt perception abstract from time, but there are also perceptions of living forms, which include their characteristic movement in time. It seems specific of living forms, that time and movement are not accidental to the Gestalt. The animal itself is such a living form, although not all animals seem able to perceive living forms like the human mind does. Humans perceive not only animals as living forms, however, but also plants and even suborganic phenomena, like a flame—all apparently active and self-controlling systems. Moreover, living forms are open systems.For the perpetuation of their life they depend, like the fire does, on an environment, and at least animals have an intrinsic relation to the environment upon which they depend, and thus to time, to the future of their own lives, although they may not be aware of that future to which their drives are related. Time, thus, is intrinsic to the living form of an animal, but it also transcends its present structure. Life, therefore, is self-transcending, and as soon as an animal becomes aware, as the human mind does, of the temporal nature of a living form, it will also perceive the transcendence of time beyond its life and death.

It is interesting that the Hebrew language produced a word which precisely conceives of this self-transcendence and indigence of the living being. The word is *näfäsh*[29] and its connotations are largely lost when it is translated as "soul." Now precisely the näfäsh, the living being in the process of its self-transcendence, is characterized in the biblical creation story as the special product of the spirit. The spirit, then, is related to form and wholeness, but more especially to the open system of the living form in the self-transcendent nature of its life process.

Do these considerations yield any result in view of our question for what the structure of a living being and the activity of the human mind may have in common, so that we may catch a glimpse of their common rooting in the spirit? First of all, the human mind perceives forms, unified wholes.

But further, the analytic abilities of the mind allow for an awareness of wholes as integrating their parts and thus of living forms that progressively integrate the elements of their lives. The mind itself has often been characterized as an integrative activity, which is nourished, however, by its analytic capacity.[30] Kant was among the first to emphasize this synthetic and dynamic character of the mind's activity. It corresponds to the structure of the life process as an open system, but now that process of continuous and self-transcending integration takes place within the field of conscious awareness, which in the more primitive forms of perception seems to be limited to the abstract forms of the environment, while on the human level these forms are perceived as wholes of parts and therefore as constituent members of a situation, of a cosmos stretching out in space and time. The human person learns to perceive his or her own body and name as located within the cosmos of its social and natural world and to perceive his or her own life as a limited process in time, together with the question for a future beyond those limits, beyond the limits of death, and for the powers transcending the objects of world as forms of their appearance. It seems to be in this self-transcending integrative process that the human mind corresponds most closely to the dynamics of life and manifests its spiritual nature, sharing in a spiritual dynamics that transcends the individual mind itself. One aspect of such transcendence of the spiritual dynamics beyond the individual is expressed when one speaks of the spirit of a community: The forms of human community are the most obvious examples (though not the only ones) for processes of spiritual integration that transcend the life of the individual. On the other hand, although each individual human person participates in the spiritual dynamics, tensions and antagonisms develop within the community life and among its individual members. How does a pneumatological scheme of human reality account for that?

In the biblical tradition, like in other archaic cultures, one is confronted with the notion of evil spirits. How it may happen that a spiritual phenomenon turns evil, becomes understandable on the basis of the integrative dynamics of spiritual processes. It is always a living form, organized around the center of self-transcendent activity and control that shares in spiritual dynamics. However, if its self-centeredness dominates its self-transcendent activity in such a way that it can no longer become a member of more comprehensive spiritual integrations, the drive towards self-transcendent integration itself becomes disruptive and divisive. Such a reflection offers a vantage point for a deeper appreciation of the early Christian differentiation between spirit and mind: Although every living form shares in the life-giving breath of the divine spirit, no form of life as such is united to the dynamics of the spirit, because in its self-centeredness every living form may turn evil. This is true even of the human mind, although—or perhaps because—in the human mind the spiritual dynamics is interiorized to the highest degree. Therefore, the human mind longs for full participation in the spirit that would satisfy his hunger for wholeness and disclose to him the nature of every creature. But the unambiguous satisfaction of such yearning is given to the mind not in the form of a definitive and exclusive possession, that the mind would inevitably surpass again, but only in the ecstasy of faith and of its hope, and in the creative love born from such faith.

PANNENBERG: *Conversations*

WHEELER: The idea that it was not mind that led to language, but language that led to mind, and this idea that we are dealing with something transcending the individual, something which reaches out into the larger community, is inspiring. And as you spoke, I could not help being reminded of that tragic story of the girl in Los Angeles who was kept confined in a room apart, until she was discovered by neighbors. Nobody ever spoke to her, she had no community, and thus, no chance of mind. Never after did she have a proper mind. This circumstance, that community develops mind, causes me to ask you, if you could think of a word better than "mind" which might capture this wonderful essence.

PANNENBERG: Well, my proposal is that the word "spirit" may be the word, and this is not far even from our present day ordinary language. Even today, however, we speak of a spirit of a community, and what is that like? It is, of course, not a substance, but it is also not the function of the sum of individuals. We have to explain individual mind as participation in this ecstatic experience, which I think the invention of language, and the use of language originally was, and all created cultural activity to the present day as being—an ecstatic experience, the sharing in the spirit of the community. And we cannot easily explain that. Because the explanation in terms of what the individuals create does not do. There is something mysterious about the reality we experience, and the poets are the first to tell us about that, about this mysterious side. I think this may be the deeper truth of the reality of our human community. What the theologians name God is involved in this phenomenon of human experience. Human community is something more than the assembly of adult individuals. They may assemble, but there is no spirit. In other cases, there is a spirit which I share.

RORTY: I don't really have a question. Perhaps I could make a couple of remarks and ask Professor Pannenberg to comment. I'm inclined to agree, almost entirely, that if we try to isolate something to be a characteristic mark of mind, then language is probably the best candidate. Like every other attempt to isolate an essence of the mental, there will be difficult borderline cases, but I think it's probably the best candidate. I also agree about the religious origin of language. It does seem an important point to make, that the pragmatic use of language is probably subsequent to the religious use of language.

On the other hand, the point at which I begin to depart from the way Pannenberg thinks about the matter comes when he raises the question "How can we explain that mind and language are fit to grasp the reality of things as they really are?" On the functionalist view of mind and of knowledge, that question doesn't arise. Knowledge, the use of language, inquiry, the development of better and better uses of language, is not a progression towards grasping the real nature of anything. It is merely a progression toward enabling us to cope with the environment, where coping is not a matter of grasping essence, but *merely* coping. That contrast permits me to make a more general point. I'm inclined to think that the notion of mind is only worth preserving in a religious context, and not worth preserving in a scientific context. If one wants a conception of man and of human knowledge such that this is a universe in which human beings are at home, a universe which is suited to them, a universe such that their minds and the objects which they wish to know are somehow connate, having a common origin, a common nature, fitting together, I suspect that only a religious conception of the universe will do. And I think that only if one has such a conception of knowledge, as a recognition of the connaturality of the knower and the known, will one have the use for the traditional notion of mind.

If one sets aside the religious attempt to see ourselves as at home in the universe, as suited to it, as planned to be members of it, and adopts the positivistic stance of Comte, and the developments which arose from Comte, then one will think of human knowledge, the relation of linguistic assertions to what they're about, in entirely pragmatic terms. The question of the relation of mind to its object won't arise. Following out that line of thought, the notion of mind itself will tend to go. One will wind up with a conception of human beings on the model of computers, black boxes, coping with what is going on around them, but not having an extra added ingredient called a mind. So I am suggesting a way of sharpening the opposition between an essentially religious conception of the universe, which indeed must hang on to the notion of mind, and an antireligious conception which in the end will be able to give up the notion of mind.

It seems to me that only if science, as we know it, transforms itself in a way which Professors Wheeler and Wigner have suggested (as, for all we know, it might), encountering entities which are much stranger than quantum indeterminancies, very strange entities indeed, might science itself lead us back towards a religious conception of mind—one which would make sense of the question "How is it that mind is fitted to grasp the reality of nature?" If that happened, then science would have led us back around to a religious outlook and away from the positivistic outlook of the nineteenth century. It seems to me that a great deal of speculation about the strangeness of the world opened up by modern science is motivated by this tendency of science. Perhaps science has a built-in direction which is antipositivistic in character. But I think that it helps, in discussing the issue of the place of mind in nature, to hold the religious conception of the relation of human knowledge to nature, and the positivistic pragmatic conception of mind's relation to its objects, as far apart as possible.

PANNENBERG: You emphasize two areas of disagreement, if I understood correctly. The first probably would require a long discussion. How can we explain that mind is fit, that we are fit, our intellectual capacity is fit to grasp things as they are. Of course, the idealistic tradition has denied that, because of the discovery of the activity of the mind. It was said that everything is appearance, everything is subjective; but on the basis of common sense we would not easily be deluded, that the world is there, and that in some way we are able to adapt to the world outside ourselves. And I think this is really mysterious. If we start on the assumption that the activities of our brain are activities, they don't receive something that is simply there. If you speak of adaptation, how is adaptation by activity possible?

The second question. I think this was a very interesting remark, that you think mind is only worth preserving as a term in a religious context. If I take this suggestion, then this is a reason for employing metaphysical language in my time period. And Karl Popper, of course, was depending on the legitimacy of using metaphysical language even in the context of science, using it as a preliminary exploration, notwithstanding the need for another kind of language—a precise, defined language that would not have the impositions of everyday language or, for that matter, of metaphysical language. And according to your suggestion, giving up the notion of mind would amount to giving up religion. Now, that is not so easy as you think. You yourself have given an example of that when you said that, in modern philosophy, the notion of mind functionally replaced the concept of God. So I remind you that in this new kind of talking, the notion of the robot may in fact replace the notion of thought—because how the robot works reminds us strongly of what Kant calls an "intuitous originalis," which is a mind that would conceive of everthing at once, not in a sequence, but it would have all of the data at once. Well, faced with the alternative to treat the rock as gold, I would rather go on with religion!

WIGNER: This was a very interesting excursion, but it is not clear to me what significance you attribute to the language. Some animals can communicate with each other to a certain degree. Do you feel that they have more spirit and more understanding than those which cannot communicate?

PANNENBERG: Some animals communicate more than others do. What about their relations with the spirit? If we look to the biblical assertions concerning the share of creatures in the divine rule there was, at this particular point, a remarkable ambivalence. On the one hand, it is said in the creation story that it characterizes the specific place of the human creature as sharing the divine spirit. But elsewhere it is said of all the animals, that they are *"näfäsh hayyah,"* a "living being" or a "living soul." All the animals then are related to the spirit of God. So in some ways there is in animals a similar being. Although obviously, at the same time in the human case, it is different. There remains an ambiguity.

WIGNER: I have a second question. If the absence of a language is the absence of spirit, I fear that it would indicate that it is not a crime to murder that girl who could not speak at all because she had no spirit and I am sure that you don't want to imply that. In fact, of course, it is quite possible that some children have some handicaps and can't easily learn a language. Should they be treated as less than human? Surely it is a crime to hurt a newborn baby even though it cannot speak. So the language is wonderful, but it is not a characteristic of man.

PANNENBERG: Well, this is a more difficult question and really a different question. When and where the human person begins. In the discussion of the pro-life people with their opponents, this is a very important question. Because I suspect there is not a point where, in the development of an individual, the person begins, and up to which point, there is no person. But we think of each human individual in terms of being a person, and this implies primarily religious elements of a dignity that should not be hurt. On these terms, a person cannot be accounted for simply on the basis of an observation that something is there, or is not there. But it is an assertion, of course, of value, an assertion of destiny. And we are convinced in our Western culture that every human individual is destined to be a person, who should not be harmed by other persons without his or her consent. But this is a statement about the destiny of human life. And in the light of this destiny, we judge the beginnings. And therefore I think there are good reasons that, in the light of this destiny, also the unborn life in the mother, it is to be called a personal life because of its human destiny.

WIGNER: In other words, it isn't a knowledge of the language which is relevant in your opinion, but the possibility to acquire the knowledge of the language?

PANNENBERG: Yes, the possibility, on account of the destiny, the disposition of a human individual to develop a full-fledged human personality.

GRANIT: All of us will remember that Descartes put this all into the pineal gland, and now Professor Pannenberg has shifted it to the language center. And so we may ask, what is really the primary thing? Cogito ergo sum or sum ergo cognito? I would like you to comment on that. I understand that you would take the Descartian position.

PANNENBERG: Well, I don't really think I shifted it to the language center, because that provides the possibility for language, doesn't it? You should answer me at this point.

GRANIT: If you say every human being has the semantic capacity and language really is the executive thing, of course, communication is very perfect in bees as you know. Bees can communicate long distances where sugar is. They can direct other bees. I wonder whether I shouldn't go to the opposite point and say that sum ergo cogito.

PANNENBERG: Without a cultural situation, a cultural setting, this capacity, this potential is not developed. I was very impressed with Heidegger's remark to this sentence of Descartes. "Well, if I have no awareness that I think, obviously I am." But how do I know that it is I that thinks? Perhaps it may be that there is some prior dim awareness that thinking is going on. And even, of course, designated that way would not be possible without the development of language which also creates in our consciousness the awareness of the "I."

GRANIT: There are, of course, these people who have lost their left half hemisphere, and there is a known case of a composer who lost it late in life. If you lose it early you can, of course, usually work up a kind of language center in the other side, but if you lose it late, why you've lost your language center. This man then, who lost that, was a great composer and he could still compose music. So there is a way of communicating without language, but which requires an awful lot of soul!

PANNENBERG: I remember a discussion of the situation of such patients by John Eccles, when he said: "Still there is a difference from the situation of prehuman living beings at first, because in the right part of the hemisphere of the brain, there are experiences collected in memories that had risen from a time when the two parts were still together; and because also the development of the right hemisphere in the human case is different from prehuman animals," although, he says, the right hemisphere works by and large in a similar way in the animal brain. Would you agree with this statement?

GRANIT: No, no I don't.

SNELL: All of us have been impressed by Dr. Pannenberg's comments on language. I also have been particularly struck by them. Dr. Wigner mentioned the capacity of animals to communicate, and I certainly think that this is an important point. It emphasizes the absence of sharp boundaries. Life is complex, existence is in a diversity of forms. I mention the whales and the porpoises. Anyone who has heard the recording of humpback whales must be impressed by the complexity of the sound they make. Now, apparently that is not as much a language in the ordinary sense as some people thought at one time, but it certainly is communication. Also, the whales and the porpoises have a remarkably supportive social structure, wherein they border on the human. But what I would like particularly to mention is that, in the matter of the evolution of language, I certainly agree with Dr. Pannenberg that the capacity to communicate is a very important driving force in the human evolution, yet it wasn't the only one. The development of the capacity to use tools was another. It was a gradual process with no cut-offs. Where did the spurt begin then? Where did self-consciousness begin? This doesn't mean these things do not exist, but I think we have to think of them in all gradations and I think that complicates the way we have to think about them. I'd like your comment.

PANNENBERG: Well, I would agree, as far as I could inform myself on these questions, that one has to consider a process that finally left a result. And in terms of that result, that is, of language as we know it, we characterize that process. While, before the process came to this result, probably it had been impossible to characterize it that way. So we have to assume, as in the development of each individual, that a process takes place in the end of which we have self-consciousness. Then we have a sense of identity, not only of objects out there, in our world, but also of identity of the individual himself or herself. And this becomes basic for that which we call mind or consciousness, for that matter.

Thus I agree that there is a process of transition that we should like to know more about. And my point in this respect was that we should not overlook the contribution of religion in the origins of the human being. The secular disciplines tend to discard questions like these, because they, in their history, departed from theology, from religion, in order to gain their independence. I think it is easy therefore that, in the phenomena that are studied, these relations to religion are excluded from the analysis. And I think the question of the origin of language in the individual as well as in society, as in culture, is an important example in case. Religion belongs very closely to the origin of the human being and the human race.

NOTES

1. Karl R. Popper and John C. Eccles, *The Self and Its Brain* (New York: Springer International, 1977), pp. 179 f. "But how could the unextended soul exert anything like a push on an extended body?" (p. 180).
2. John Locke, *An Essay Concerning Human Understanding* (New York: Dover, 1959), II, 23, 5.
3. David Hume, *A Treatise on Human Nature*, 2d. ed., L. A. Selby-Bigge (1739/40; reprint eds., Oxford: Clarendon Press; New York: Oxford University Press, 1978), pp. 232 ff., 250; cf. pp. 251 ff.
4. Cf. Popper and Eccles, *The Self and Its Brain*.
5. Ibid., pp. 56 ff.
6. Ibid., pp. 22 ff., esp. pp. 27 ff.
7. Ibid., pp. 12 f.
8. Ibid., p. 73 and p. 13, cf. p. 30 ff.
9. Ibid., p. 109.
10. Ibid., p. 115, cf. pp. 554 ff.
11. Ibid., pp. 437 ff., esp. pp. 441 ff. Eccles is much more hesitant to attribute consciousness to animals, even to primates; cf. pp. 518 ff and 534 f.
12. Ibid., p. 38; cf. the remarks on language as a "tool" pp. 48 f.
13. J. Locke, *An Essay Concerning Human Understanding*, II, 23, 18, and 15.
14. Ibid., II, 23, 5.
15. Augustine, *De lib. arb.*, I, 8, 18: . . . hoc quicquid est, quo pecoribus homo praeponitur, sive mens, sive spiritus, sive utrumque rectius appel-

latur . . . Ratio ista ergo, vel mens, vel spiritus cum irrationalis animi motus regit, id silicet dominatur in homine cui dominatio lege debetur ea, quam aeternam esse comperimus. Cf. *De Trin.*, XIV, 16 (CCSL 50a), 453, 35 ff. Usually, Augustine prefers to speak of mind *(mens)* of reason *(ratio)*. That may be explained by the semantic complexity of the term spirit (see the diverse meanings enumerated in *De Gen. ad litt.*, XII, 7 f. and *De Trin.*, XIV, 16) or also by the danger of mistaking the term spirit for the divine spirit: To this see *De Gen. c. Manich.*, II, 8 and also *De Gen. ad litt.*, VII, 2 ff. Perhaps it is not by accident that the anthropological discussions of his work on the Trinity do not refer to Gen. 2:7 except in the passing remark, II, 18, 34.

16. Thomas Aquinas, *Summa theol.*, I, 97, 3c: . . . anima rationalis et anima est, et spiritus. Dicitur autem esse anima secundum illud quod est commune ipsi et aliis animabus, quod est vitam corpori dari . . . sed spiritus dicitur secundum illud quod est proprium ipsi, et non aliis animabus, quod silicet habet virtutem intellectivam immaterialem.

17. Ibid., I, 36, 1c: nomen *spiritus* in rebus corporeis impulsionem quandam et motionem significare videtur; nam flatum et ventum spiritum nominamus. Cf. Augustine *De Trin.*, XIV, 16 (CCSL 50a, 452, 32 ff.).

18. Immanuel Kant, *Anthropologie in pragmatischer Hinsicht* (1798), p. 57 *(Anthropology from a Pragmatic Point of View*, trans. Mary J. Gregor [The Hague: Nijhoff, 1974]); F. W. J. Schelling, "Ideen zu einer Philosophie der Natur" (1797), in *Werke*, ed. K. F. A. Schelling, pp. 2, 51. Cf. Georg Marquardt, "Art. Geist," in *Historisches Wörterbuch der Philosphie* (1974), ed. J. Ritter, Vol. 3, pp. 184 f., 186 f. According to Marquardt, this romantic conception of Geist combines the aesthetics of genius and theology (p. 187 f.). For the post-Hegelian reduction of spirit to the individual consciousness, see pp. 199 f.

19. Cf. Walther Zimmerli, *Ezekiel* (1969), Vol. 2, p. 895; cf. p. 900 (*Ezekiel-One*, trans. Ronald E. Clements, ed. Frank Moore Cross and Klaus Baltzer [Philadelphia: Fortress, 1979]). When Zimmerli, p. 895, distinguishes the conception of Ezekiel from Eccl. 12:7 in that in the word of the prophet the *ruah* does not come from God, but is called from its presence in the world, this is a correct description of the vision itself (cf. Ezra 37:9), but Zimmerli's remark does not do full justice to the explanation, where the breath of life is explicitly related to the spirit of God himself (Ezra 37, 14).

20. See Wolf-Dieter Hauschild, *Gottes Geist und der Mensch: Studien zur frühchristlichen Pneumatologie* (1972), pp. 30 ff., 36 ff. (for Clement), pp. 89 ff. (Origen), pp. 152 ff. (Gnostics), pp. 201 ff. (Tatian), pp. 206 ff. (Irenaios).

21. Ibid., pp. 41 f. (Clement).

22. According to E. Cassirer, *Philosophie der symbolischen Formen* (1923–1929), Vol. I, pp. 56 f. (*Philosophy of Symbolic Forms* [New Haven: Yale University Press, 1953–1957]), this is characteristic of the mythical conception of language, while the differentiation of language from this arises from the reflection that in language the object is only represented, but not itself present (II, p. 53).

23. J. Piaget: *Nachahmung, Spiel und Traum* (1975), pp. 116 ff., 127 ff., 310 ff., 316 ff.

24. Julian Jaynes in his presentation "The Evolution of Language in the Late Pleistocene" at the New York Congress on *Origins and Evolution of Language and Speech* (New York, 1976, pp. 312–325, esp. 319) assumes a close interrelation of the origins of language, art and religion. And Susan K. Langer conjectures, that the festive celebrations of early cultic ritual may have provided the occasion for the first development of language (*Mind: An Essay on Human Feeling* (1972), II, pp. 303 ff., 307 f.).

25. Karl Rosenkranz: *Der Ursprung der Sprache,* 1961, pp. 112 f., 114 ff. See the opposite argument in: A. Montague, "Toolmaking, Hunting and Language." In *Origin and Evolution of Language and Speech,* New York, 1976, pp. 266–274).

26. Popper and Eccles, *The Self and its Brain,* pp. 1–35.

27. G. Sübmann, "Geist und Materie." In H. Dietzfelbinger and L. Mohaupt, eds., *Gott-Geist-Materie: Theologie und Naturwissenschaft im Gesprach,* Hamburg 1980, pp. 14–31, p. 20: "So erscheint uns der Stoff aller Dinge wie aus Gedanklichem gewirkt."

28. Ibid., pp. 22 f.

29. See Hans Walter Wolff, *Anthropologie des Alten Testaments* (1973), pp. 25–40 *Anthropology of the Old Testament,* trans. Margaret Kohl [Philadelphia: Fortress, 1974]).

30. Together with Karl Popper, John Eccles belongs to those who follow C. Sherrington in recognizing the decisive characteristic of the human mind in the integrative unity of consciousness (1.c.524, cf. Popper and Eccles, *The Self and Its Brain,* p. 127). But Eccles relates the integrative activity of mind directly to the vast plurality of neural cells, modules and centers in the brain. From his insight that "the unity of conscious experience comes not from an ultimate synthesis in the neural machinery," he concludes that it must be placed "in the integrating action of the self-conscious mind on what it reads out of the immense diversity of neural activities in the liaison brain" (p. 356). According to Eccles, the mind selects from "the multitude of active centers at the highest level of brain activity" (p. 362) and "from moment to moment integrates its selection to give unity even to the most transient experiences" (Ibid., cf. pp. 478, 488). But in fact the mind does not know of "brain events," except for a rather late stage of human research. The integrative activity of the mind is related to momentary perceptions and memories, not to brain events. The synthesis of brain events in the momentary perception ("a unified conscious experience of a global or Gestalt-character") is operating on another level than the integrative activity of the reflective mind. That Eccles—in contrast to Popper—does not properly distinguish between consciousness and self-consciousness (the self-conscious mind) becomes also evident in his dialogues with Popper on the origin of consciousness (cf. above n. 11).